Group Communication

D0064389

How does group membership influence individual behaviour? In what ways do groups change and develop? How do different groups relate to one another?

Group Communication provides an introduction to the theories and practical applications of small group dynamics. Drawing on concepts from social psychology, linguistics and communication studies, Peter Hartley shows that an understanding of how groups work and interact will improve the chances of successful team communication and co-operation.

Group Communication includes:
- critical reviews of group research
- explanation of the difficulties and practicalities of observing groups
- analysis of major group processes, including conformity and decision-making
- analysis and case studies of the management team, student seminar/project groups and self-help groups
- practical recommendations for group communication
- references and suggestions for further reading and research

Peter Hartley is Senior Academic in Communication Studies at Sheffield Hallam University, and was one of the team which developed the first British undergraduate degree in this area. He teaches theoretical and practical courses in interpersonal and group communication to a wide range of students, managers and other groups, using the ideas in this book and *Interpersonal Communication* (Routledge, 1993).

Group Communication

Peter Hartley

London and New York

First published 1997
by Routledge
11 New Fetter Lane, London EC4P 4EE

Simultaneously published in the USA and Canada
by Routledge
29 West 35th Street, New York, NY 10001

© 1997 Peter Hartley

Typeset in Times by J&L Composition Ltd, Filey,
North Yorkshire
Printed and bound in Great Britain by T.J. International Ltd,
Padstow, Cornwall

British Library Cataloguing in Publication Data
A catalogue record for this book is available from the British
Library

Library of Congress Cataloging in Publication Data
Hartley, Peter
    Group communication/Peter Hartley.
        p.   cm.
    Includes bibliographical references and index.
    1. Communication in small groups.   I. Title.
    HM133.H365   1997
    302.3'4—dc20   96–34698

ISBN   0–415–11159–5
         0–415–11160–9 (pbk)

Contents

Acknowledgements   vii
Introduction   ix

Part I

1 Why bother – why study small groups?   3
2 What are we talking about? Definitions and differences   19
3 Ways of observing and analysing what goes on in
   groups   33

Part II

4 How do groups change and develop?   53
5 How are members influenced by the group?   71
6 Who wants to be leader?   88
7 Who does what? Structure and communication   112
8 And the answer is . . . group problem-solving and
   decision-making?   131
9 When groups collide – enter the intergroup   156

Part III

10 Getting groups to work – teams in organisations   177
11 Groups can help us learn – teamwork and students   189
12 Groups can help – groupwork and some final thoughts   202

Index   219

Acknowledgements

To my primary group: Julia, James and David. Special thanks to Julia for patience and support when deadlines loomed; to James for fixing the lawnmower and solving other life mysteries; and to David for regular concern and encouraging noises, especially 'how many words have you done now?'

To many groups and individual students who have listened and questioned, especially Roma Eastwood and the last few Totley generations.

To colleagues who have supported my ramblings on these topics, especially over the last year or two: Kathy Doherty, Mark Neath and Maddie Smith.

To Rebecca Barden and colleagues at Routledge for patience and consideration beyond the call of duty.

This book is an affectionate tribute to two very different social groups who have been important to me:

- To all former group members who shared collective dreams and fantasies, especially the Vikings, the Cleveland Warehouse Gang, and Sounds Four.
- To all past and present members of Darnall Medical Aid.

This book is dedicated to the memory of Tony Linley. He will be remembered among many things for his loyal and selfless contribution to all the groups he joined.

Introduction

If one or more of the following situations is familiar to you, then you should find this book both interesting and useful.

Now we'll form into groups and . . .

You are a student at school or college attending the first class of one of the most important modules. The lecturer explains that the main task for the module will be a group project with most of the marks being awarded for the quality of the group product. To give every group an even start, the groups have been compiled by a random choice from the list of names.

How do you feel about this? Are you looking forward to meeting a new set of people? Are you worried that you will have to spend so much time getting along with them that this will detract from the quality of the work you will get done? Are you worried that the others might be much more committed than you and expect you to put in too much time and effort? Are you worried that one or more members of the group might refuse to take groupwork seriously and fail to pull their weight? Are you worried that you might have to lead the group? Are you worried how this project will affect your final marks?

And the management team for this new project is . . .

Your organisation has decided to support a new project which is very dear to your heart. A project group has been established and has been given six months to carry out a feasibility study. If this is successful then this could lead to a new department being set up, which could provide a major new career opportunity for you. You have been nominated to serve on the project group.

How do you feel about this? Are you looking forward to working with a new set of people? Are you worried that you will have to spend so much time getting along with them that this will detract from the quality of the work you will get done? Are you worried that other members of the project team might not be as committed as you are and might refuse to pull their weight? Are you worried that you might be asked to chair the meetings? Are you worried that there might be competition between members of the project group in anticipation of the next phase of the project?

And the agenda for today is the agenda for today . . .

You are one of the management team in your organisation or division. You are attending the first meeting of the team with your new boss. She suggests that one of her priorities is to improve the effectiveness and efficiency of the management team. Next week, the team will spend a day at a residential centre on a team-building exercise. This is likely to be the first of many days of this type of training.

How do you feel about this? Are you looking forward to this new way of working which emphasises team co-operation? Are you worried that you will have to spend so much time getting along with the team that this will detract from the quality of the work you will get done? Are you suspicious or welcoming of this type of training? Do you feel that it might be a waste of time as the group members are not motivated to change their behaviour? Are you worried that there might be one or more members of the group who refuse to take this initiative seriously and do not pull their weight?

What we need is an action group to sort out City Hall . . .

Proposals for a new out-of-town shopping and leisure complex have horrified you and other residents of the nearby village. You know that this will kill most of the local shops and dramatically increase through traffic, threatening the quality of life in the village. After a meeting of local residents, you have been elected to lead the protest group and the first meeting is tonight.

How do you feel about this? Are you looking forward to working with this set of people? Are you worried that you will have to do too much? Will you be able to rely on others to pull their weight? Are you worried that the group might not be able to sort out its priorities and degenerate into conflict? Are you worried about your role as leader and what the other members might expect of you?

What this book can offer

In all these situations, you are thrown together with a collection of people whom you may not know very well which is expected to become a cohesive and productive team (sometimes overnight). The success of any of these ventures will depend upon how you and your companions wrestle with the problems of group dynamics. And that is the main theme of this book – how we can use theory and research into group dynamics to highlight difficult areas and find ways of improving the chances of successful group communication and co-operation.

Some books on group or team performance are full of practical hints and tips, the implication being that these hints all work every time. Unfortunately, life is not like that! We *do* know enough about the complexities of human behaviour to know that there is no single strategy or technique which is guaranteed to have the same effect on everybody. We also *do not* know enough about all the different varieties of everyday groups to be confident that all our recommendations will be sensible. As a result, this book offers insights into a number of relevant research studies and theories, not just for the sake of stimulating the mind but because theory is useful in suggesting what might be the most likely outcomes of any given practical situation.

So my main aim in this book is to provide an interesting and accessible introduction to the analysis and practical implications of small group dynamics. I have drawn main concepts and theories from social psychology but have also wandered elsewhere through the social sciences when necessary. All the concepts are explained in a way which does not assume that you have already studied social science.

Of course, you cannot develop your group skills just by reading this book:

Any individual working with groups can only become proficient by receiving feedback on his or her performance, which is then used to upgrade that performance.[1]

What this book can give you is ideas on how groups might be succeeding or failing and what types of behaviour might be appropriate in a given group. You can also use some of the concepts to identify what might be useful feedback. As no one book of this size can provide a really comprehensive review of the subject, I have included specific references on all the major topic areas so you can explore further if, like me, you have become fascinated by the complexities of human beings in social groups.

Writing this book has helped me to think about the way that I behave in, and relate to, groups which are important in my social and work life. I hope that you will find it as useful.

How is this book organised?

The major sections

Part I provides some of the justifications and background for the study of group dynamics. Chapter 1 starts to answer the 'why bother?' question by demonstrating the influence of group processes in important decisions. The value and limitations of group research is illustrated by debating the value of brainstorming. Chapter 2 looks at how we can interpret different definitions of the term 'group' and shows how group membership is both an important part of how we see ourselves and how we decide to behave. Finally, it provides a model which categorises different levels and types of group interaction. Chapter 3 investigates the issues of how we can observe and interpret behaviour in groups by looking at a selection of different schemes and theories which have been used in major studies.

Part II examines group processes in more detail. Each chapter is organised around a major question or issue which we need to answer to arrive at a useful understanding of how groups interact. Each chapter also contains discussion of the practical applications and implications of the ideas and techniques discussed. For example, in Chapter 4 – How do groups change and develop? – we examine theories and studies which suggest that small groups have a 'life cycle' and go through a predictable series of stages or changes. Understanding these changes is important if we want to help a group make the most of its resources. The remaining chapters each take a major area and explore both theory and practical applications: social influence, leadership, group structure and roles, group problem-solving and decision-making, and communication across group boundaries.

Part III looks at specific areas where we can apply the theories and techniques described in Part II, including the management team (Chapter 10), the student seminar and project group (Chapter 11), and self-help and personal development groups (Chapter 12). Finally, Chapter 12 highlights some important unresolved issues which affect this area, brings together some of the most important themes, and suggests some likely developments to take us into the twenty-first century.

Within chapters

Each chapter is organised to reflect the statement of aims given at the beginning. At the end of each chapter, there is a list of notes which provides:

- details of references cited in the text
- further comments for anyone wishing to explore the topic in more detail
- references and suggestions for further reading

What is the best way to read this book?

This text will be read by many different people (I hope) with different aims in mind. Depending on your approach, I suggest the following strategies: If you are reading because you are particularly interested in the practical applications of group theory, then I suggest you:

- read Chapter 1 to get some background
- skim Chapters 2 and 3 and/or read them later
- read all the relevant chapters in Part II
- read relevant sections of Part III

If you are reading this as a student on a course, then I suggest that you:

- read all Part I first
- read subsequent chapters in the order in which they crop up on your course
- when you read a chapter, skim-read it first then go through it more slowly and check the notes

Language and sexism

In my own teaching, I warn students to avoid sexist language and expressions. So I have tried to practise what I preach. In this book, 'he' is always 'male' and 'she' is always female. Where I quote from authors who are not so careful, I try to clarify their use of language.

For anyone who is not convinced that sexist language should be avoided both for the sake of accuracy and fairness or who would like help on how to avoid it, I recommend immediate reading of Miller and Swift.[2]

Notes

1 This very appropriate advice comes from page 4 of the book by Tom Douglas, which offers an analysis of group processes from the perspective of group members. There is useful discussion of practical examples which you can use to complement the analysis in this book:
Douglas, T. (1995) *Survival in Groups: The basics of group membership*. Buckingham: Open University Press.
2 For a very comprehensive analysis and practical handbook on how to avoid sexism in language: Miller, C. and Swift, K. (1989) *The Handbook of Non-Sexist Writing*, 2nd edn. London: The Women's Press.

Part I

Chapter 1

Why bother – why study small groups?

This chapter explains the importance of group analysis by showing how 'faulty' group interaction and communication can lead to disastrous consequences. Such disasters are not inevitable. Group communication can be improved and this demonstrates the practical value of group analysis – we can use the analysis to identify problems and modify our communication to improve group effectiveness.

Unfortunately, we cannot simply rely on common sense to provide the right recipe for effective groupworking. This is illustrated by comparing views from the advocates and critics of brainstorming, one of the most popular suggestions for helping groups to become more 'creative'.

These examples establish some of the main themes in this book: the need to carefully examine what is going on in groups, the practical value of group analysis, and the pitfalls of believing that we currently know all the answers.

Group decisions and group processes: one group that went astray!

Groups can make poor decisions. These can be avoided if the group pays more attention to the way they work together. To illustrate this principle and to show how the analysis of group communication can have a very clear practical pay-off, I will use a dramatic and tragic real-life example. I have been scaring successive generations of students with this example of a group who went disastrously wrong since it was first publicised as part of a British television documentary on the causes of civil aviation accidents.[1]

The recording of the flight crew's conversation survived the crash and provides a grim reminder of what can happen when a professional group fails to monitor its own processes.[2] The plane is only 8 miles from its destination and the Captain has misjudged his landing approach – he is flying 40 knots too fast and 200 feet too low. The Co-pilot has been checking the instruments and realises something is wrong – the dials indicate that the plane is flying too low. Ideally, the Captain and Engineer should have checked this out. But this is not what happened in the subsequent conversation – I have numbered the comments so I can refer back to them later.

1 CO-PILOT: Below the glide slope there, John.
2 CAPTAIN: Well, we know where we are; we're all right.
3 ENGINEER: The boss has got it wired.
4 CO-PILOT: I hope so.
5 ENGINEER: Right on.
6 CAPTAIN: Oh yeah. No problem.
7 CO-PILOT: Isn't this a little faster than you normally fly this John?
8 CAPTAIN: Oh yeah, but it's nice and smooth. We're going to get in right on time. Maybe a little ahead of time. We've got it made.
9 CO-PILOT: I sure hope so.
10 ENGINEER: You know, John, do you know the difference between a duck and a co-pilot?
11 CAPTAIN: What's the difference?
12 ENGINEER: Well a duck can fly.
13 CAPTAIN: Well said!

A pause of several seconds.

14 CO-PILOT: Seems like there's a little bit of a tailwind up here, John.
15 CAPTAIN: Yeah, we're saving gas – helps us to get in a couple of minutes early too.

Another pause.

16 CO-PILOT: John, you're just a little below the MDA here.
17 CAPTAIN: Yeah, well we'll take care of it here.

The next few minutes are taken up with the routine pre-landing checks. The tone and pace of the conversation changes dramatically when the crew no longer have to rely on the instruments and can see the landing field directly.

18 CO-PILOT: Really look awful high, John.
19 CO-PILOT: John, you're really high. You're gonna need 40 here.
    It's what you need here to get this thing down.
20 ENGINEER: You want the speed brakes on?
21 CO-PILOT: I don't think you're gonna make it, John, if you're
    gonna get this sucker on the ground.
22 ENGINEER: Get it on, John.
23 CO-PILOT: You're not gonna make it.
24 CO-PILOT: You're not gonna make it.
25 CAPTAIN: We're going round.
26 CO-PILOT: You're not gonna make it, John.

The Captain was unable to rescue the situation at this point. Ironically, the last words on the flight recorder came from the Co-pilot: 'Right, John, I told ya, Jees!'

At first sight, it might seem almost impossible that a highly trained professional team could make such a disastrous and elementary blunder. And yet the television programme went on to highlight a significant number of accidents where the main cause was the poor co-ordination of the flight crew. The American airline involved revised their training programmes for flight crews to place more emphasis on their group skills rather than just their technical expertise.

Before reading on, you might like to go back through the cockpit conversation and identify what you think were the problems in communication and interaction which contributed to this tragedy.

So who was to blame?

One response to an accident of this type is to try to assign blame or responsibility to the individuals involved. The Captain is clearly in charge and would take ultimate responsibility for the decisions made during the flight, but does this mean that the other crew members were in no way responsible? Was it not the lack of true co-operation and teamwork which created the real problem? This was the argument which persuaded the airlines to change their training and recruitment practices. It is only by analysing the group process and communication that you can see what went wrong and how it could have been avoided. Consider the following factors, all of which are important themes running through the rest of this book.

Team processes and procedures

There is no real sense of the crew working as a team. The initial query from the Co-pilot (comment 1) is quickly dismissed. The following comments provide the first of several examples where the the Engineer and Captain 'gang up' on the Co-pilot. The clearest example is the Engineer's rather feeble joke (comments 10–13). In the last minutes of the flight, the Engineer and Co-pilot seem to be piling extra pressure on the Captain rather than supporting his attempts to rescue the situation (comments 21–26).

Style of leadership

The Captain was taking a very clear line that he was in charge and was unwilling to accept any challenges to his expertise. Again this is illustrated by his response to the very first query from the Co-pilot where he seems to make no attempt to check the situation regarding the glide slope. An autocratic style of leadership ('do as you are told') can be very powerful.

Status and communication style

Airline crews have a very clear formal hierarchy, rather like military organisations. The Co-pilot has a relatively low status in the formal pecking order and he seems to respond accordingly. Contrast the style of communication used by the Co-pilot – hesitant, indirect, apologetic – with the confident, dismissive style used by the Captain. If you ever have the opportunity to see the programme, you can see how this is reflected in the nonverbal signals – tone of voice, hesitations – used by the two characters. Low status members of groups often find it difficult to make their views heard by the other members.

Influence and conformity

The Engineer made several comments to put himself 'on the side' of the Captain (comments 3,5,10,12). The Co-pilot was confronted with a unanimous majority which he was unable/unwilling to defeat. He felt obliged to conform.

Role and personality relationships

One problem uncovered in the investigation into incidents like this accident was that the typical pilots recruited by the commercial airlines of this period were ex-fighter pilots. These individuals tended to have a characteristic personal style which was well suited to solo work – individualistic and competitive – but could be counter-productive when it came to managing a team. The personality did not really match the role demands.

Of course, we have no way of knowing whether this particular team had any awareness of their own limitations in teamwork. The important outcome was that the airline involved used the results of this sort of analysis to make major changes to its training programmes. Flight crews were tested and trained in skills of communication and co-ordination as well as their technical expertise. So this dramatic incident highlights the importance of effective group dynamics in situations where the consequences of decisions can be the difference between life and death. And problems like this are not inevitable – teams can improve their processes and procedures.

Of course, we must also be aware that most real-life situations are influenced by a range of factors and group dynamics is only one of those factors. For example, there may have been additional factors at work among the flight crew. Many accidents of this type have been related to fatigue and stress, especially when the participants are working complex shift patterns which can upset natural body rhythms.[3]

Relating to other groups and situations – a word of caution

The importance of teamwork in problem-solving and decision-making is apparent in a whole range of situations, and I shall highlight many of these in later chapters, including the government policy group, the jury, the management team, and the student project group.

There have also been several other important studies of groups involved in catastrophes which we can use to highlight issues of group process. For example, the Challenger disaster in 1986 has received attention from several researchers. The explosion of the Challenger space shuttle shortly after take-off received world wide media coverage. When the cause was identified as the failure of rubber seals which had been affected by the unusually adverse weather, many people wondered how such a sophisticated organisation as NASA could fall foul of a problem which should have shown up in simple safety checks. Detailed accounts of the events show a very complex sequence of communication and decision-making which was affected by both group and individual factors.

The potential problem with the seals had been identified some time earlier by an engineer. His warnings were initially ignored. The unusually cold weather did prompt officials to review the launch conditions but again the warnings about the seals were not acted upon. The final launch was sanctioned by an individual who was apparently unaware of the various engineers' reservations as his team had not made him aware of the conflicting opinions. Researchers suggested that the disaster was the result of 'a complex interplay among a number of cognitive, psychological, and social forces constituting the decision environment'.[4] Among the factors identified were faulty beliefs held by important groups, faulty reasoning, perceived pressure by groups and individuals, ineffective persuasion, and use of ambiguous language.

However, we also need to be cautious when we try to extrapolate from studies of group interaction into our own everyday situations. For example, Diane Vaughan has provided the most recent and possibly definitive account of the events leading up to the Challenger disaster.[5] She suggests that there were further dimensions to this situation which were not fully appreciated either by the presidential commission investigating the disaster or by subsequent researchers. Rather than being the consequence simply of poor communication or of managers violating specific rules to comply with pressures to make the launch, she concludes that the disaster was a consequence of the organisational culture which had developed in NASA, a culture which adopted a particular view of potential dangers. The dominant view that developed in that culture was that the risk associated with the suspect joints was an acceptable one and that the mission was therefore safe. Thus the actions of groups and individuals in the situation were a reflection of the dominant culture which had developed over a number of years. Vaughan talks about the 'normalisation of deviance' which took place at NASA: 'The decision to launch resulted from NASA's institutionalised process of normalising signals of danger.' As a result of this culture, participants seemed to 'lose sight' of the true riskiness of the technology they were dealing with. This 'slippery slope', where there is a gradual and incremental shift in beliefs and attitudes, can affect large and small organisations and we shall see similar patterns of behaviour in some of the other research later in this book, notably in some of the studies on conformity. The main lesson from this analysis is that we must always take into account the history, culture and ideologies within which groups operate.

Research into groups has tended to focus on either experimental situations (often using undergraduate students as the subjects) or case studies of situations where it is possible to interview participants and use documentary evidence, as with the Challenger disaster. As a result, we do not have sufficient accounts of everyday groups working in 'non-dramatic' situations to be certain that some of the processes identified in these group studies really do affect us all. So I must insert a word of caution – regard the proposals in this book as hypotheses about group behaviour which have been shown to work in some situations but which need further checking and testing.

For example, there is insufficient work on how groups operate when they contain members from very different cultural backgrounds and yet this is now the norm in my student groups and in many work situations. One recent study suggested that groups with members from one culture – monocultural – felt and behaved very differently to multicultural groups.[6] Monocultural group members were very similar in the rules they accepted for leadership behaviour in groups. Multicultural group members subscribed to a range of different opinions. As a result of these stronger shared norms, the monocultural groups were able to behave more flexibly in *this* situation.

Similarly, we do not really know enough about the differences between male and female interaction in small groups although there is an increasing focus on potential differences between male and female behaviour in social situations. For example, recent research has suggested that all-male groups will contain conversations on more impersonal topics with one person holding the floor at any one moment; all-female groups will focus on more personal topics and feature overlapping talk, where two or more members join in a single speech either by emphasising or by 'filling-in' details. This overlap is not competitive whereas overlapping speech in male groups is usually an attempt to gain the floor at the expense of the original speaker.[7]

Even some of the classic studies referred to in this book are still searching for really adequate explanations, perhaps because at the time when they were carried out the importance of cultural variables was not fully recognised.

Common sense is not enough

One common accusation levelled at social science research is that it is just common sense heavily dressed up with scientific jargon. But can we rely on common sense to explain how people interact in groups? You will not be surprised if I argue that common sense is insufficient. There is now considerable research evidence which challenges popular common sense views about social life.[8]

Before using a case study to illustrate why we need much more systematic knowledge of group processes, I have a few logical reservations about purely relying on a common sense approach:

Whose common sense do you use?

One of the common features of common sense is that there is a saying to suit every occasion, and these are often contradictory – 'many hands make light work', cf. 'too many cooks spoil the broth'.

Common sense may be limited

Would not a common sense approach suggest that aircraft flight crews should always adopt a professional and problem-solving approach? At the very least, surely they would always pay attention to potential problems when there was potential danger involved?

Common sense may ignore important factors

Suppose you are a tutor or teacher and you know that one of your students is lonely. Should you put that person in with a group of students to help them overcome their loneliness? I have explained this situation to many people and they have agreed that this would be an sensible, 'common sense' tactic. Unfortunately, I can cite more systematic research which suggests that this could be exactly the wrong approach.[9] My student may be feeling lonely because he feels dissatisfied with the quality of his interaction with other people. Putting him in with a group without any preparation may simply give him more opportunity to feel dissatisfied and inadequate. The only really effective strategy would be to give him some social skills training *before* he enters the group so he has a chance of developing some successful relationships.

However, I am *not* suggesting that personal experience is invalid or useless and I shall discuss this later when I identify some of the weaknesses and limitations of group studies. For the moment, I shall use the example of brainstorming to illustrate why and how we need detailed studies of group processes, and how current research may be incomplete.

The value of brainstorming?

Brainstorming is possibly one of the most 'misused' words in describing group interaction. The term was coined to describe a very specific group technique. However, you will often hear people say they are going to brainstorm when all they do is have a normal discussion which tries to suggest some new ideas.

The specific technique of brainstorming was first proposed by Osborn in 1957,[10] and was developed to overcome some of the common difficulties that groups face when having to solve problems. These problems are discussed in some detail in my chapter on group decision-making. For the moment we simply need to concentrate on the proposition that the use of brainstorming helps groups become more creative.

There are two very general principles behind brainstorming: first that problem-solving is best done in stages and, second, that each stage should obey certain rules. There are three main stages – the first is the generation of ideas. All ideas generated during this stage are recorded for later consideration. The usual format is to have someone to lead the session who can enforce the rules and act as a scribe. This stage should also have a definite time limit, say 10 minutes. During this time, everyone in the group must obey the following:

No evaluation

While the group is brainstorming, no-one is allowed to criticise or evaluate any of the ideas being expressed. This means no negative comments and no other forms of judgment, such as shaking heads.

No censorship

All ideas are acceptable. No suggestions are to be rejected, no matter how fanciful or bizarre they may appear at first sight. You are encouraged to suggest ideas which break some of our normal taboos.

Quantity of ideas

You are encouraged to produce as many ideas as possible in the given time. The emphasis in this brainstorming stage is on producing quantity of ideas. The judgment of quality is made at a later stage.

Hitch-hike

You are encouraged to hitch-hike, i.e. to build upon the ideas that have been suggested by others in the group.

After the time limit is up, each idea is looked at in turn to see if it is worth pursuing.

If you have not experienced brainstorming before, try it out with a group of friends or colleagues. Remember to set a time limit in advance, follow all the rules and record all the ideas. After you have done the brainstorm, work through all the ideas one by one and decide which are worth pursuing. You may also want to collect reactions to the method from the other members of the group before you read the next sections of this chapter. Did everyone follow the rules? Did everyone participate fully? Did everyone feel that the group came up with useful ideas? Would you be happy to use the method again?

Does brainstorming 'work'?

This question is difficult to answer, and also demonstrates some of the problems of undertaking social research. How would common sense evaluate brainstorming? Doesn't it sound a useful and enjoyable procedure for encouraging creativity? How would you measure its effectiveness?

You can certainly find positive summaries of this technique from practitioners, alongside enthusiastic endorsement in some textbooks:

> [brainstorming] rules, when enforced by the leader of the group, overcome many of the roadblocks to creative thinking. Ideas will flow much more freely when blocks to creativity are eliminated.[11]

Unfortunately, if you review some of the more detailed research, a much more complicated picture emerges. Other commentators are not convinced about the value of brainstorming:

> The irony of brainstorming is that it is most frequently used where research suggests it is least effective.[12]

> Osborn claimed that groups which follow these instructions generate more ideas, and that the (subsequently assessed) quality of these ideas is also superior. However, the empirical evidence does not support this claim.[13]

So can we resolve this difference of opinion with more systematic research? Consider some of the following findings and issues:[14]

- The effectiveness of brainstorming depends upon previous experience and training. Participants may need practice to become familiar and comfortable with the rules. How easy is it to train groups to the point where they feel really comfortable with this method?
- It is difficult to guarantee that no self-censorship takes place. How much effect does this have?
- If you compare a group of four people in a brainstorming group and four individuals working on their own for the same period, many studies have found that the four individuals will produce more ideas between them. The quality of the ideas produced by the individuals may also be rated more highly than the group's. This raises the issue of what you compare brainstorming groups with to arrive at a fair comparison – do you compare them with groups working with other methods or with individuals working on the same problem?
- Do we have adequate measures of the quality of ideas as opposed to just the quantity of ideas?

If brainstorming is not necessarily as effective as first claimed, how do we explain this? Some writers have cast doubts on the fundamental assumption behind brainstorming, namely that people will think creatively if they think there are no obstacles to producing a 'free-floating' torrent of ideas.[15] Others have suggested three main processes which can explain why these groups are not more effective:

Free riders

Individuals in brainstorming groups will be aware that all the ideas are pooled and so there is the temptation to relax and let others do more of the work.

Evaluation apprehension

Brainstorming is intended to reduce the anxiety of having your ideas evaluated and criticised, but it cannot guarantee that individuals automatically lose any concerns about others' reactions. If you are apprehensive about the reactions/evaluations of other members, then you will tend to limit your contributions.

Production blocking

Only one member can speak at a time – other members must wait their turn. This obviously limits participation and may mean that other members either forget or lose track of their ideas.

All of these possible explanations have been investigated, usually concluding that blocking is the most significant problem.[16] Other factors such as group size also appear to be important influences.

Can we therefore conclude that brainstorming has been over rated as a technique and is not worth the effort? This conclusion might be premature as you can also be critical of some of the research:

- What social effects does the technique have? Does brainstorming help a group to develop good team work in a more general sense? If so, then it may be justified even if it is not the most 'efficient' way of generating ideas.
- In experimental studies, the tasks may not have any real significance for the group members. Does brainstorming work differently when the group is engaged on a task which the members feel is really important? Or could this work the other way – the more important the task, the more limited the value of the technique?

Most of the studies have neglected both of these issues – they have used experimental designs with individuals and groups who have been assembled for the occasion, working on interesting problems but not ones which had any real significance for the group members. In contrast, many of the claims for the effectiveness of brainstorming seem to rely on anecdotal evidence, highlighting examples where groups seem to have come up with a really exciting new idea which has made a major impact.

Can brainstorming 'work'?

I cannot provide a definitive conclusion on the practical value of brainstorming for a given situation because of the complexities highlighted above. In fact we may never see the research programme which would be necessary to arrive at a definitive answer. Who is going to pay researchers to investigate a large sample of 'real' applications of the brainstorming technique in industry and education?

However, there are a number of studies which suggest that we cannot discount the potential value of techniques like brainstorming. One study found that:

> with the introduction of a minimum of structure, group brainstorming performance improved dramatically.[17]

Perhaps some of the negative studies have implemented brainstorming in too 'free and easy' a fashion. They may also have neglected to bring participants fully 'up to speed' with the method. A study of the impact of training in 'Creative Problem Solving' (CPS) suggested that fully trained groups demonstrated more participation, less criticism, more support, more use of humour, and more ideas than untrained groups.[18] There was also more even participation in the trained groups.

Of course we are still confronted by the problem of explaining the effects we observe. If a working group regularly use brainstorming and find it effective, can we automatically conclude that this is due to the method? Or are there other group processes which are more important?

For the moment, the systematic research that is available relies on experimental investigations. These certainly demonstrate that brainstorming will not necessarily guarantee the most creative solutions. However, we must remember the limitations of these studies. Of course, you can use the results to suggest variations/improvements to the process, such as using smaller groups, or asking members to write their ideas down individually. Some of these ideas have been used in other problem-solving methods which are also discussed in my chapter on group decision-making.

There is another intriguing recent development. A number of researchers have used the brainstorming method with computerised formats. Rather than produce the ideas face to face, group members are at individual workstations connected through a computer network. In this situation, brainstorming can outperform both real groups and the pooled contributions of individuals working alone. Performance is especially improved for larger groups with more than twelve people.[19]

Back to the point

The main point of this exploration into brainstorming was to show how we need careful and systematic analysis of group processes. We cannot simply rely upon common sense. On the other hand we must ensure that any research is both comprehensive and valid. Where research does suggest that the picture is more complex, we need to be clear on why and how we are using specific techniques.

For example, under what conditions is it appropriate to use a brainstorming group? I will continue to use brainstorming groups because they can have important social effects – they can act as an 'ice-breaker' to help a group develop more of a co-operative spirit. They can also produce good ideas, especially when a group has tried other ways and is getting 'stuck' on a particular issue. But they are not a magic solution which will guarantee success.

Notes

1 The documentary was *The Wrong Stuff*, first broadcast on BBC2 in February 1986. The programme examined a series of aeroplane incidents which were attributed to pilot error and reviewed NASA's work, following a report reviewing 50,000 comments from flight crew members since 1975. The NASA Research Centre in California went on to use a simulator to recreate dangerous incidents and observe how these were handled by experienced flight crews. They observed many situations where crews were confronted with ambiguous and/or unreliable information and did not have the team skills to resolve this ambiguity successfully.

2 See Rupert Brown's book (p. 91ff.) for an analysis of this incident in terms of social conformity: Brown, R. (1988) *Group Processes*. Oxford: Blackwell.

3 For a full analysis of the possible effects of these sorts of problems (and what we may be able to do about them), see: Moore-Ede, M. (1993) *The 24 Hour Society: The risks, costs and challenges of a world that never stops*. London: Piatkus.

4 The Challenger explosion is used by Robert Feldman as the prologue to his chapter on group processes (Chapter 14) in his textbook on Social Psychology, which gives a recent account from an American perspective of many issues covered in this book. The quote is taken from the opening synopsis of the article by Hirokawa *et al.* which provides a detailed analysis of the incidents leading up to the launch: Feldman, R. S. (1995) *Social Psychology*. New Jersey: Prentice Hall; Hirokawa, R. Y., Giuran, D. S. and Martz, A. E. (1988) Understanding the sources of faulty group decision making. A lesson from the Challenger disaster. *Small Group Behaviour*, 19, 411–33.

5 A useful summary of Diane Vaughan's research can be found in Davies' article. The quotes are taken from the article: Davies, J. (1996) Risk in the rules. *Times Higher Education Supplement*, 22 March, p. 22; Vaughan, D. (1995) *The Challenger Launch Decision: Risky technology, culture and deviance*. Chicago: University of Chicago Press.

6 This study is: Zamarripa, P. O. and Krueger, D. L. (1983) Implicit contracts regulating small group leadership. *Small Group Behaviour*, 14, 187–210.

7 These examples are taken from recent research by Jennifer Coates. For a recent (and controversial) analysis of male–female differences in communication which has achieved best-selling status in the USA, see the book by Deborah Tannen: Coates, J. (1996) *Women Talk. Conversations between women friends*. Oxford: Blackwell; Tannen, D. (1994) *Talking from 9 to 5*. New York: William Morrow.

8 For discussion of many examples, see: Furnham, A. (1996) *All in the Mind: The essence of psychology*. London: Whurr.

9 You may like to read this article and decide how far you can generalise these findings: Anderson, C. M. and Martin, M. M. (1995) The effects of communication motives, interaction involvement and loneliness on satisfaction. A model of small groups. *Small Group Research*, 26, 118–37.

10 Osborn's original claims for brainstorming can be found in: Osborn, A. F. (1957) *Applied Imagination*. New York: Scribner's.

11 In their chapter on The Communicating Manager as a Decision-Making Problem Solver (Chapter 13), Rasberry and Lemoine point to studies which support the value of brainstorming, p. 361ff.: Rasberry, R. W. and Lemoine, L. F. (1986) *Effective Managerial Communication*, Boston: Kent

12 This quote is taken from a short article by Adrian Furnham. He argues that individuals perform better than groups on poorly structured, creative tasks which is where brainstorming groups should have the advantage. He then quotes a 'recent study' using the 'moon survival' problem (see Chapter 8) which does not really lend itself to brainstorming!: Furnham, A. (1992) Can brainstorming cloud the collective mind? *New Scientist*, 31 October.

13 Wilke and Meertens provide a useful summary of the main experimental studies on brainstorming (pp. 36–41): Wilke, H. A. M. and Meertens, R. W. (1994) *Group Performance*. London: Routledge.

14 For a typical modern summary of brainstorming from a management point of view, see: Huczynski, A. A., and Buchanan D. A. (1991) *Organizational Behaviour. An introductory text*. 2nd edn. London: Prentice Hall.

15 See note 14.

16 See note 13.

17 This study is: Hart, S., Borough, M. and Enk, G. (1985) Managing complexity through consensus mapping: Technology for the structuring of group decisions. *Academy of Management Review*, 10, 587–600.

18 For a description of these comparisons and for further details on CPS, see: Firestein, R. L. (1990) Effects of creative problem solving training on communication behaviours in small groups. *Small Group Research*, 21, 507–21.

19 For a recent study which suggests that electronic brainstorming can work, see: Connolly, T., Routhieaux, R. L., and Schneider, S. K. (1993) On the effectiveness of brainstorming. Test of one underlying cognitive mechanism. *Small Group Research*, 24, 490–503.

Chapter 2

What are we talking about? Definitions and differences

This chapter investigates what we mean by a group and presents the argument that a psychological group is *much more* than just the sum of the individuals within it. This is illustrated by reviewing different definitions and classifications of 'groupness' which show the variety of processes we can expect to find. These definitions have practical implications as they highlight the factors which are necessary to maintain a group over time.

This chapter also introduces the issue of how our personal relationships relate to our membership of social groups – membership of social groups is a fundamental component of our personal identity. This can have both positive and negative consequences.

The chapter introduces several models which you can use to reflect upon group processes and also introduces issues of observation and analysis which are discussed in Chapter 3.

The meaning of 'groupness'

One of the most long-standing arguments in social psychology (and more generally in social science) concerns the 'reality' of social groups. Perhaps this is best understood as a question – in order to understand how and why a group behaves, do we need to know anything more than the personal characteristics of the group members? In other words, is a group anything more than simply the sum of its component parts? For example, can we make an analogy with the properties of water? You cannot work out the characteristics of water simply by knowing all about hydrogen and oxygen which are its two components. It is the way that the molecules of hydrogen and oxygen combine that gives water its distinctiveness. Is this also the case with people – that there are properties of social groups which cannot be predicted simply by adding together the characteristics of the component individuals?

One of the main arguments in this book is that a group *is* more than the sum of its component parts. There are group processes which can be outlined and which do not simply depend upon the characteristics of the individual group members – being accepted as a member of a group has psychological consequences which in turn can change the nature of the individual.[1] Perhaps the clearest illustration of this is the development of group norms which are produced through the social interaction of the group but then act as a frame of reference for the individual members. Consider the discussion of group norms in Chapter 5 – such norms could not possibly emerge unless the members were responding to a concept of the group as real. This takes us into the problem of definitions – deciding which characteristics are really important when defining a group.

Investigating the definitions

This is not as simple an issue as at first appears. For example, if you review the definitions used in a range of social psychology textbooks, you will find a number that emphasise different aspects of behaviour in groups.[2] There are four common types of definition you will find:

- **Common fate**: there are definitions that emphasise the fact that members of a group typically share a common fate.
- **Social structure**: there are definitions which focus upon the social structure of the group.
- **Interaction**: there are definitions which focus upon the nature of the interaction which takes place between members of a group.
- **Categorisation**: there are definitions which highlight the fact that members of a group define themselves as members of that group. In other words, in order to be a member of a group, the important thing is to see yourself as a member of that group.

If we have a variety of definitions with different emphases then can we find one characteristic which is crucial? The one characteristic I would emphasise and which is critical in many of the studies covered in this book is categorisation – the perception or definition by individuals that a group exists and that they are or are not members. The way people think about their social situation is the decision on which other variables depend. So the simplest definition of a group is that offered by Rupert Brown – that a group exists when:

> people define themselves as members of it and when its existence is recognised by at least one other.[3]

Take the implications of this a bit further and you arrive at the definition offered by Tajfel and Turner who see a group as:

> a collection of individuals who perceive themselves to be members of the same social category, share some emotional involvement in this common definition of themselves, and achieve some degree of social consensus about the evaluation of their group and of their membership in it.[4]

This adds notions of emotional attachment and evaluation to the categorisation – both important aspects of the value that we attach to the groups we are in. There are also some other variables which we cannot ignore.

Group size

Are two people a group? You will find definitions of groups which suggest that two people can act as a group. This assertion is vigorously rejected by many authors including myself. In the jargon of psychology, a pair of people is often called a dyad. The interaction in a dyad can be very different to the interaction expected in a group. For example, it is not possible to have any sub-groups when you only have two people, but this is a very important group dynamic. However, you can suggest that size is an important variable in groups. When you increase the size of a group certain processes become more or less likely, e.g. the likelihood of sub-groups increases, as does the need for leadership.

Social and cultural variations

Most books on group dynamics have come from the USA. Have they adequately reflected the possible variations in group interaction which you might find in other cultures? For example, in a recent review of the relationships between leadership, organisations and culture, Smith and Peterson[5] found much more consistent relationships between leadership style and group productivity in Japan than in the UK or USA. They suggest that this may be due to cultural variables but also warn that the meaning of what may appear to be the same act will differ across cultures. The boss who regularly checks on your work can be seen as considerate or intrusive, depending on the meaning and value attached to this behaviour.

Group boundaries

How can we draw the boundary lines between different groups? Look back to the list of groups that you are a member of. At any one time, which group are you a member of? What happens in a situation where you are aware of more than one group membership? For example, suppose you are a member of a longstanding discussion group, and you are a committed Christian. Suppose the discussion topic is leadership. If the discussion turns to church leaders and other members of the group start to raise major doubts about these leaders' ethics and competence, which loyalty is uppermost in your mind? If you do experience some conflict of loyalty, what do you do about it? For example, do you remain silent in order not to risk antagonising other members of the group?

The dimensions of small groups

Another approach to defining groups is to identify the characteristics which make some groups differ from others. There are a number of useful proposals along these lines:

Categories of group interaction

Rather than look for the ideal definition, many authors have tried to outline the main categories of group interaction. For example, Henri Tajfel and Colin Fraser argue that groups have six major characteristics, listed in Table 1.[6]

One way of applying these characteristics is to present them as dimensions. Different groups will have a different profile on these characteristics. See Figure 1.

The profile of group A suggests a group with a strong sense of itself and very good relationships between the members. Group B meets fairly regularly and the personal relationships are good but there is not a very strong organisation or sense of purpose. This might be typical of a casual friendship group.

Table 1

Characteristic	What it means
Interaction	Group members interact with one another in different ways.
Perception	Group members see themselves as members of the group.
Goals	The group has particular purposes or goals. Of course, these goals may not be explicit. For example, a friendship group will have the goal of enjoying itself and supporting each other. These goals are unlikely to be discussed.
Norms	The group will have specific norms, i.e. specific ways of behaving which are accepted and followed by the group members.
Roles	Group members will take on different roles. We shall discuss this in detail in Chapter 7.
Affective relations	The group members will like each other to varying degrees.

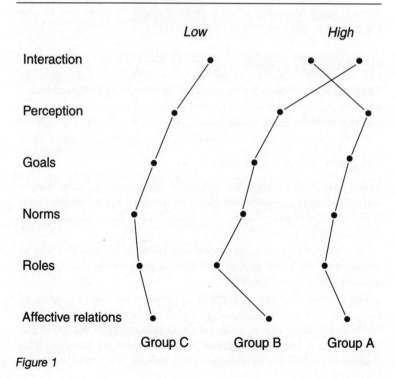

Figure 1

One practical consequence of this model is that we should not think of groupness as an 'on-off' characteristic: is C a 'red' group? There is no magic moment when a collection of people turn themselves into a psychological group. Rather we should think of degrees of groupness defined in terms of these dimensions. Some of the group phenomena explained in this book are only likely in groups which show significant degrees of all these dimensions.

Levels of interaction

An alternative way of categorising groups in general is to identify different levels of group interaction. One common distinction is made between group content and group process. Group content includes all the jobs, activities or tasks which the group is undertaking. This is the 'what' of group interaction. Group process refers to 'how' the group operates, and this covers the relationships between the members and how they deal with one another.[7]

Classifying group processes

Group definition can also be achieved by looking at ways of classifying the major processes that you will find in groups. Tom Douglas has provided a classification into four categories as shown in Table 2.[8]

The basic category is interaction, without which the group could not exist. The structural category includes all the 'group-building'

Table 2

Category	What is involved
Basic	Interaction
Structure	Group development
	Social structure
	Sub-group formation
Movement	Decision-making
	Purpose
	Goal formation
Molar	Formation of norms
	Development of cohesion
	Influence and group pressures
	Development of climate

processes. The processes in the movement category are all those processes which move the group towards its objectives. The molar category includes overall and less specific processes which group members will recognise but find difficult to define.

Different types of small groups

Finally, group definition can be achieved by suggesting that there are different types. Again there are a number of ways of classifying types. For example, Tajfel and Fraser[9] distinguish four main types: family groups, friendship groups, work groups, and laboratory groups. These are fairly self-explanatory except for this last category. Laboratory groups are groups assembled for the purpose of participating in a psychological experiment. As so much of the material on group dynamics is based on experiments with this sort of group, it is worth investigating their characteristics more closely. The typical group will be young American undergraduates, often all the same sex, who do not know each other beforehand. They will only meet for an hour or two. As a result, I would share Tajfel and Fraser's conclusion that such groups are

> hardly groups at all. More charitably we could argue that many small-group studies are, in fact, controlled studies of only the very earliest phases of group development.[10]

For this reason, the studies which receive most attention in this book are those which have focused on groups in more naturalistic settings.

There are a few more points to make about this list of types:

- **The changing family**: the composition of the typical family group has certainly changed in the last few decades in the UK and USA with the increasing rates of divorce and single parenting.
- **The changing work group**: there are also changes in the typical work group. Recent attention to so-called 'team-based' organisations will be discussed in Chapter 10. Some researchers have suggested that the type of work groups now found in large organisations are a relatively new invention. For example, Meredith Belbin, whose work on team roles is featured in Chapter 7, suggests that the way teams are now used in organisations represents a new form of social organisation, quite different

from traditional models of boss–subordinate relationships.[11] This argument is examined in Chapter 10.

- **New self-study groups**: the last thirty years has also seen the advent and rise of another new type of group: the self-study group – a group who meet regularly for the purpose of either exploring group dynamics or their own personal development in a group context. A brief history of this development and its impact is provided by Peter Smith[12] and we discuss it in Chapter 11.

What do groups mean to you?

If you want to participate in a social psychological study, take a blank piece of paper and write down at least 20 answers to the following question – 'Who am I?'

This procedure was originally devised by Kuhn and McPartland[13] to study how people defined themselves. They found that nearly everyone gave at least one group reference in their answers and most gave more than half. What groups did you select? How important are they to you?

If you consider your range of answers to this question, you have provided some evidence of your self-concept. The model of the self-concept which I will use at several points in this book is based upon the social identity approach. Key features of this model are explained below:

- Your self-concept is made up of all the descriptions and evaluations which you apply to yourself. For example, if you have nothing else to do, you could go on answering the 'Who am I?' question until you ran out of descriptions to apply to yourself.
- The self-concept is not just a random list or catalogue of all the ways you can describe yourself. It is organised in particular ways.
- Your self-concept has 2 different sub-systems – social identity and personal identity. Each of these sub-systems contains descriptions and evaluations which are organised in 'self-identifications'.
- Your social identity contains social identifications which derive from membership of specific social categories, e.g. mine would include lecturer, male, white etc.
- Your personal identity contains personal identifications. These identifications are your individual characteristics which are not

based on group membership. For example, you may see yourself as happy, enthusiastic, positive etc.

This may seem rather abstract and theoretical. In fact, this definition of the self-concept has very real implications for the way we behave. It suggests that we categorise ourselves into social groups. It also suggests that we use different self-identifications in different circumstances. These ways of categorising ourselves have very real consequences for our behaviour. This can be illustrated with a few examples.

We meet in another universe

One of my answers to the 'Who am I?' test is 'lecturer'. I see myself as a member of that professional group within this society and this does not just affect my life within the confines of the job. Suppose you are a student and we happen to meet at the annual party of the Uppertown Star Trek Enthusiasts' Society, an organisation which I was sure did not have any members drawn from my work life. My normal behaviour in the Society is not based on my lecturer identity but based on my personal identifications – happy, enthusiastic, creative etc. – and my conformity to the group norms such as adherence to Federation rules etc.

Apart from being taken aback by the authenticity of my Klingon make-up, you will immediately confront the dilemma of how to relate to me in that circumstance. I will have the same problem. We can talk to each other on the basis of our newly discovered link as Trekkies, or as individuals having a good time, but will we ever be able to completely forget the other social identities, especially if we both know that next week I'll be marking your final assignment?

We need to negotiate

A similar dilemma in terms of identity would occur if we needed to negotiate in some formal capacity. Suppose we were close childhood friends who happened to work for the same large company, but in very different areas. What happens if we then meet as management and union representatives respectively on a negotiating committee to resolve a dispute over staffing levels? And what if the resolution of this dispute will almost certainly lead to some redundancies? Assuming that the roles of representative are important parts of our self-concepts, we have to decide how to behave. We cannot behave 'as friends' to each other in this situation. Will both relationships survive? The conflict in situations like this can often kill personal relationships.

These examples were hypothetical. They introduce an important distinction between interpersonal and group behaviour – the factors involved are very different and this is highlighted when we consider circumstances where members of different groups meet. When we communicate with another person on an interpersonal basis we act in terms of our and their individual characteristics; where we communicate with another person on a group basis, we act on the basis of our group memberships. This distinction is not either/or but is a matter of degree. It has been described as the interpersonal–group continuum and is summarised in Table 3.[14]

This suggests that the there is a continuum running from the interpersonal end to the group end. So we are either in an interpersonal situation or a group situation. Unfortunately this dichotomy is too simple. In many situations we are aware of both dimensions at the same time and adjust our action accordingly. This is of particular importance in the study of communication across group boundaries which is the focus of Chapter 9.

Where group identification leads to self-destruction

If the group identification is very strong, this raises the issues of whether it can be too strong – can a group then become too cohesive for its own health? This is an issue which crops up on several occasions later in the book, e.g. in Chapter 5. We can certainly

Table 3

Factor	Interpersonal	Group
Awareness of social categories/group memberships	Low	High
Uniform behaviour and attitudes within one group	Low	High
Stereotyped perceptions of members of other groups	Low	High
Uniform behaviour towards other group members	Low	High

identify many real examples where the processes of group identification have had a very dramatic impact on the individuals involved:

Suicide and schoolchildren

As I was planning this chapter, I heard a radio news feature which was investigating the increasing number of Japanese schoolchildren committing suicide. We shall see later that the Japanese do seem to put greater emphasis on group loyalty than the British or Americans. The radio report concluded that the increase was attributable to a corresponding increase in bullying and other pressure from classmates. The children could not bring their distress out into the open for fear of losing face and betraying other members of the group. As the reporter remarked 'the power of the group is overwhelming'.[15]

Cults can kill

There are a number of well-documented cases where cult groups, usually with a very charismatic leader, have decided to either commit mass suicide or launch a plan of action which was guaranteed to bring about their destruction.

An integrative model

One general model which I have used to start people thinking about how groups operate suggests that there are three fundamental levels of analysis needed to fully understand group interaction, as in Figure 2. Problems can arise at any or all of these levels and usually involve a mix of factors.

The interpersonal underworld

This refers to the pattern of likes, dislikes, admirations, resentments and all other emotional attachments which exist between the group members, some of which may have subconscious roots. Many self-development groups aim to explore this level of functioning and make it a main topic of discussion – many, if not most, everyday work groups will do just about anything to avoid discussing it openly!

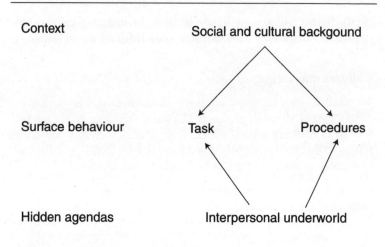

Context   Social and cultural backgound

Surface behaviour   Task   Procedures

Hidden agendas   Interpersonal underworld

Figure 2

Task and procedures

This is the level of overt organisation of the group – the task it has been set or has set itself (which could be simply having a good time) and the procedures it adopts (the way it organises itself in terms of how members communicate, take on roles etc.).

Context

This includes the social and cultural background, both in terms of the group members and also in terms of the setting in which the group is operating. For example, Zander[16] has produced a fascinating comparison of Japanese and American groups. He suggests that the values of co-operation, group loyalty and pride in the group's achievements are far more important to the Japanese than individual rewards or responsibilities. Alongside this is the belief that explicit conflict and disagreement must be avoided and that you should avoid embarrassing or hurting others even if it means concealing your own feelings. The American way is diametrically opposed, encouraging individual responsibility and advancement and encouraging open communication and expression of disagreement. Translate these different values into small group interaction and you have very different behaviours and expectations. Members of the two different cultures will not be able to interpret each others' behaviour adequately without some knowledge of these values.

Cultures and ideologies

We shall suggest on many occasions throughout this book that you cannot expect all small groups to behave in the same way. One final way of classifying groups which aims to deal with this and which relates to this notion of culture is the attempt by Hinkle and Brown[17] to classify groups in terms of two different dimensions:

Individualism–collectivism

An individualistic culture emphasises individual independence from groups; a collective culture emphasises co-operation and group loyalty.

Competitive or uncompetitive

The main focus of a competitive group like a sports team is competition with other groups, whereas a jury or a therapy group is unlikely to be concerned with other groups.

Putting these two dimensions together suggests four main varieties of groups which will react differently to similar situations. For example, a competitive/collectivist group – the very cohesive sports team – may be much more susceptible to the processes of social influence explained in Chapter 5 than a group where individualist/uncompetitive values are dominant.

Notes

1 For a full analysis of this argument and a detailed comparison with other positions, see the first chapter of: Turner, J. (1987) *Rediscovering the Social Group*. Oxford: Blackwell.
2 For further definitions and more discussion on the issue of the reality of groups, see Chapter I of Susan Wheelan's book and pages 121ff. of Augostinos and Walker: Augostinos, M. and Walker, I. (1995) *Social Cognition. An integrated introduction*. London: Sage; Wheelan, S. A. (1994) *Group Processes. A developmental perspective*. Boston: Allyn and Bacon.
3 From pages 2–3 of: Brown, R. (1988) *Group Processes. Dynamics within and between groups*. Oxford: Blackwell.

4 From page 15 of: Tajfel, H. and Turner, J. C. (1986) The social identity theory of intergroup relations. In Worchel, S. and Austin, W. G. (eds) *Psychology of Intergroup Relations*. Monterey, CA: Brooks/Cole. pp. 7–24.

5 See pages 96ff. in: Smith, P. B. and Peterson, M. F. (1988*) Leadership, Organizations and Culture*. London: Sage.

6 See in Chapter 7 of: Tajfel, H. and Fraser, C. (eds) (1978) *Introducing Social Psychology*. Harmondsworth: Penguin.

7 For an alternative discussion of the content-process distinction, see Chapter 4 of: Douglas, T. (1995) *Survival in Groups: The basics of group membership*. Buckingham: Open University Press.

8 See in pages 52ff. of: Douglas, T. (1979*) Group Processes in Social Work: A theoretical synthesis*. Chichester: John Wiley.

9 This discussion is based on Tajfel and Fraser, pages 181ff. (note 6).

10 This quote is from Tajfel and Fraser, page 181 (note 6).

11 See the discussion in: Belbin, R. M. (1993) *Team Roles at Work*. Oxford: Butterworth Heinemann.

12 For a useful history and review of these groups, see: Smith, P. B., (ed.) (1980) *Small Groups and Personal Change*. London: Methuen.

13 This is originally described in their 1954 article. For a more recent review of work using this simple technique, see the book by Zurcher. Kuhn, M. H. and McPartland, T. S. (1954) An empirical investigation of self attitudes. *American Sociological Review*, 19, 68–76. Zurcher, L. (1977) *The Mutable Self: A self concept for social change*. Beverly Hills, CA: Sage.

14 The interpersonal–group continuum was developed by Henri Tajfel.

15 From a report by Philip Short on the Radio 4 *Today* programme, 20 December 1994.

16 Alvin Zander has written extensively on groups and social issues. This comparison is from a 1983 article: Zander, A. (1983) Groups in Japan. *Small Group Behaviour*, 14, 3–14.

17 See their article in: Hinkle, S. and Brown, R. J. (1990) Intergroup comparisons and social identity: Some links and lacunae. In Abrams, D. and Hogg, M. A. (eds) *Social Identity Theory: Constructive and critical advances*. Hemel Hempstead: Harvester Wheatsheaf. pp. 48–70.

Chapter 3

Ways of observing and analysing what goes on in groups

This chapter examines different ways of observing and interpreting how people behave in groups, contrasting methods which use a category scheme to identify behaviours as they occur with methods which depend upon theories of the human subconscious and unconscious mind.

Suggestions are then made about how we can use ideas from these approaches to make sense of our own and others' behaviour as we participate in groups.

What methods are there?

This chapter will not provide you with a comprehensive list or analysis of every method available to study group interaction. Rather the purpose is to highlight major issues which need to be resolved if you want to make some close analysis of a group. To achieve this, I shall contrast two main approaches which operate from very different premises: one approach which is based upon observation and classification of the members' overt behaviour, and another approach which is based on extensive interpretation of what is going on. Members' behaviour has to be interpreted in the light of unconscious or subconscious processes.

As a result, I shall ignore for the moment other methods although these will be mentioned in later chapters (also see note 10). For example, I shall not discuss ethnographic methods which rely on participant observation – the researcher joins the group and aims to see the group interaction through the eyes of its members. There are several important studies using this method. They all have to come to terms with the issues discussed in this chapter – how do we interpret the behaviour of those around us?

What do the members do?

One way of analysing group behaviour is to try to categorise and record everything that the members do. There have been many attempts to develop category systems which are both valid and usable. One of the most popular methods for recording group interaction and communication (Interaction Process Analysis – IPA) was first developed in the 1950s by Robert Freed Bales.[1] It is worth examining how Bales derived this model from basic principles as you can then see (and question) the assumptions on which this approach is based. These basic principles had important influences on the way that a great deal of social research was conducted in the 1950s and 1960s.

Bales proposed three basic ideas about groups which are fundamental to understanding his work.

The small group is a social system

What this suggests is that we can discover all the major processes which occur in social systems by investigating small groups. This was a very important idea in the 1950s and partly explains the popularity of small group research in those days. Obviously, it is much easier to study a small group than it is to study a large community or society. If the processes are much the same, then small group research is both useful and effective. Needless to say, this model has been disputed. Most researchers today would be much more cautious about how far you can generalise their findings.

There are fundamental issues which every group must resolve

The first distinction here is between what Bales called the task area and the social emotional area (analogous to the content-process distinction used in the last chapter). You can then break down each of these areas into a series of problems. In the task area, there are problems of communication, evaluation (working out which ideas to accept and which to reject) and control (keeping up to date with the task demands). In the social emotional area, there are problems of decision (how members show agreement and disagreement), tension reduction (whether members are joking, laughing and using humour) and reintegration (how members show solidarity and support others).

Table 4

Area	Positive	Negative
Socio-emotional	1. Shows solidarity	12. Shows antagonism
	2. Releases tension. (jokes, laughs, etc.)	11. Shows tension
	3. Agrees	10. Disagrees
Task	4. Gives suggestion	7. Asks for orientation
	5. Gives opinion	8. Asks for opinion
	6. Gives information	9. Asks for suggestion

We can observe and classify group behaviour on these lines

Bales identified six major problems. Each of these has a positive and negative side. For example, when we communicate we can either give information or ask for information. So this gives us 12 categories (as listed in Table 4) and Bales used these 12 categories to develop a system for observing behaviour in groups which was then used in many important studies.

The numbers in Table 4 are the category numbers which Bales used, i.e. 'shows solidarity' is category 1; 'shows antagonism' is category 12.

How IPA works

An act is defined as 'the smallest meaningful and discriminable piece of behaviour which an observer can detect'.[2] The problem is, of course, deciding what to count: we must include all the varieties of non-verbal communication,[3] and any one utterance can contain a number of acts. For example, how would you code the following remark from a group member?

> Mm, I don't know, maybe. Why don't we sort this out now? I think we should discuss this and ask what help the library are going to offer.

Try using the Bales categories on this extract before you consider my analysis in Table 5.

There are a number of acts in here as follows: there are also a number of potential sources of ambiguity:

- Does the initial 'Mm' signify agreement or disagreement? I have taken it to register understanding or acceptance which is category

Table 5

Utterance	Category
Mm	3
I don't know	10
Maybe	3
Why don't we sort this out now?	4
I think we should discuss this	4
and ask what help the library is going to offer	4

3. The non-verbal tone is needed before you can really decide here.

- Is the 'maybe' part of the 'Mm' or not?
- Is the final sentence one or two proposals?

And this is before we start on the nonverbal accompaniment to the speech. One thing this does demonstrate is that you cannot just pick up the system and apply it without any further preparation. Bales always puts his observers through a rigorous training scheme until they can demonstrate that their coding is as consistent and reliable as experienced observers.

How has IPA been used?

IPA has been used in a wide variety of contexts, and studies have reported some important and consistent findings, including:

- that larger groups are more likely to be dominated by a single individual
- that different individuals use different patterns of the coding categories which reflect the roles they take on in the group
- that different types of group have different patterns of acts. For example, children's groups seem to include more negative socio-emotional acts
- that the pattern of acts can change our time. For example, in a problem-solving group, you are likely to find more informational acts in the early parts and more positive socio-emotional acts later on

It can be used to give a group an independent account of what it is doing which may surprise group members. For example, in a recent research project I was involved in, we used IPA to record the meetings of case conferences used in social work.[4] These are meetings to decide what should happen to children who have been taken into care and are attended by a whole range of professionals including social workers, probation officers etc. Under a new policy initiative, parents were allowed to attend part of the meeting on the grounds that this would enable them to provide more information about their circumstances and their perceptions. The analysis of the meetings and the patients' interactions suggested that this was not happening. Without any briefing or preparation for the meeting, parents were unable to contribute to the situation in the way that was intended, which is not too surprising when you consider that they were confronted by the very professionals who they were in conflict with. The analysis also suggested that the role of the chair was critical – either involving or shutting out the parents from the discussion.

We later came across a study of multidisciplinary teams involved in medical case conferences, which used very similar methods.[5] This also emphasised the importance of the chair role. The chairs were usually consultants and therefore high-status members – they tended to dominate the meetings. There were also clear differences between chair as the task leader and a social/emotional leadership role taken on by one of the other members.

What IPA cannot provide is the impressions and interpretations of the group members themselves. This was incorporated in Bales' later system – SYMLOG – which is summarised below.

From IPA to SYMLOG

IPA has been widely used and is summarised as the 'standard' coding interaction coding system in virtually every social psychology textbook. By contrast, Bales' later system, the System for the Multiple Level Observation of Groups (SYMLOG) is often not mentioned and seems to have been little used by other researchers.[6] SYMLOG categorises acts within groups on three dimensions:

- forward/backward refers to behaviours which are either towards or against the group goals
- positive/negative refers to behaviours which are friendly or unfriendly
- upward/downward refers to behaviours which are either dominant or submissive

This obviously requires much more interpretation by the observer but it also includes a method for comparing the observer's perceptions with the participants'. Group members are asked to rate each other on an adjective rating scale which can then be analysed, using the same three-dimensional structure.

One other outcome of this method is a graphic representation of the group showing each member's position on the three dimensions. These positions will indicate some important aspects of the group's operation. For example, close clustering suggests a very cohesive group; where the group members fall into two sub-groups clustered in different areas, there is likely to be significant group conflict.

There are several possible reasons for the relative lack of research interest in SYMLOG: it is much more complex than IPA; it first appeared at a time when group-dynamic research had become less popular; and it does not pay much attention to the content of the group task. Instead, researchers have been keener to develop category schemes which are tailored to the specific social situation they are investigating.

Difficulties and issues

As SYMLOG has not made a major impact, it is worth returning to IPA and assessing the main difficulties and issues with a category system of this type. There are a number of major issues:

The categories may be too global

As the categories are designed to cover each and every situation, they may not distinguish between acts which should really be seen as distinctive in a particular situation. For example, verbal and nonverbal expressions of support may both express support but have every different connotations in the same situation. As one critic puts it:

> the very global nature of the categories blurs too many vital distinctions and lumps together too many aspects of the interactive process that ought to remain distinct.[7]

The verbal/nonverbal difference

You may get very different results if you use a video or live coding which enables nonverbal signals to be taken into account, compared with coding a verbal transcript.

No judgement of intensity

There is no scale of intensity for the categories in IPA. For example, showing tension release will cover everything from a mild snigger to a loud guffaw.

Cannot we just add categories?

Of course this is possible but this will increase the problems for the observer. Can you keep track of say eighteen categories rather than twelve?

Reliable and valid?

Can the categories be applied consistently by different observers? Do the categories provide valid descriptions of the underlying behaviour?

Other classification systems

If you start from different basic assumptions or with different overall purposes, you can end up with a very different set of categories. To illustrate these differences, I will use two very different examples: Danziger's functional analysis,[8] and Heron's six-category intervention analysis,[9] and then try to bring out the main ideas they have in common.

Danziger's functional analysis

Based on his criticisms of Bales, Kurt Danziger developed what he called 'a system for analysing rhetorical codes in conflict situations' which can be used in interpersonal and group situations.[10] He adopted a functional perspective which means that:

> we must base the classification of verbal utterances on the role that they play in the social interaction within which they occur.[11]

Like Bales he starts from first principles by deciding that there are four basic functions of human communication – 'to teach, to please, to move, and to defend oneself'.[12] In other words, we communicate to inform, to satisy our emotional needs and develop friendships, to make things happen and to justify our actions by responding to any perceived attacks or criticism.

This classification is then used to generate twenty-nine categories but these are not presented as a list as in Bales. They are organised in a tree diagram or algorithm so that the coder works down the tree until reaching the category which fits the utterance. For example, consider the statement 'Is this OK with you?' This would be categorised by Danziger using the following steps:

- the first level of the algorithm is the choice between a relevant and irrelevant utterance. An irrelevant statement is one that does not contribute to the group task – it is coded as such and is not broken down any further.
- relevant statements are subdivided into objective and non-objective statements. An objective statement is a simple statement of fact about the outside world – 'it's starting to rain'. As our speaker wants some response from others, it is what Danziger calls non-objective.
- non-objective statements are subdivided into assertions or demands. We decide that our statement is a demand.
- demands can be imperatives or requests. Our example is a request.
- requests can be orientation or confirmation. Our example is orientation which is coded as act 2500.

This may look very cumbersome when expressed in this way but is of course much easier and quicker when you have the tree diagram in front of you and have practised using it.

Although this system does not seem to have been used very extensively, it shows how you can build a category system from first principles and also highlights one of the main problems – how observers must interpret the actions they see. Danziger explicitly codes acts as relevant or irrelevant and in effect dismisses irrelevant acts. As you will see from some of the other theories we confront, deciding which acts are really relevant to a group's progress is not straightforward by any means.

Six-category intervention analysis

This was developed by John Heron over a period of years and is primarily focused upon group leader behaviour.[13] It has been used extensively in the analysis of group facilitators, running self-

Table 6

Mode	Category	What the leader does
Authoritative	1. Directing	Suggests what is to be done
Authoritative	2. Informing	Gives information
Authoritative	3. Confronting	Disagrees, questions or gives feedback
Facilitative	4. Releasing	Jokes, helps members express emotions
Facilitative	5. Eliciting	Draws out members' contributions
Facilitative	6. Supporting	Approves members' contributions

development groups of various kinds (these groups are discussed in Chapter 12).

Heron proposes six categories which fall into two main groups: authoritative and facilitative. When leaders are in authoritative mode, they act in dominant and assertive ways; when they are in facilitative mode, they are helping the group move along either by improving the group climate or by supporting the interaction between members. Categories 1–3 are authoritative; categories 4–6 are facilitative.

One interesting aspect of this scheme is that it only codes behaviours which are seen as desirable and worthwhile. It does not include behaviours which Heron regards as negative or destructive. Within each category there are more specific skills which Heron believes good group leaders should display. For example, as a form of eliciting, leaders can 'echo'. This is the act of echoing back to a member the last few words they have said as a way of encouraging them to speak more and expand on what they have said.

Common themes and issues

Although the category schemes explained above are very different in many ways, there are common themes and issues which are relevant to anyone who decides to observe and classify group interaction. Of course, there are also many other schemes which have been used to study groups[14] and these also share a number of important concerns:

The nature of acts

All category systems have to decide on their 'unit of observation'. How far are we chopping up the behaviours in order to decide what to categorise?

The nature of interpretation

On what basis are we interpreting the behaviour we observe. For example, the phrase – 'that's a good idea' – can be delivered as a straightforward compliment or as deep sarcasm. How easy is it for an external observer to recognise these nuances?

Verbal and nonverbal behaviour

We cannot ignore noverbal behaviour but how do we code it?

Comprehensive or specific

Do we need a global scheme like Bales or are we focusing on particular behaviours which are important to the group in its specific situation?

Positive, negative or both

Are we including behaviour we regard as negative or unhelpful, as well as positive and helpful acts?

We shall return to some of these issues later after inspecting a few methods which try to look beneath the surface of group behaviour.

Looking beneath the surface: what are the hidden anxieties which determine what members do?

A very different picture of group interaction appears if you adopt a theory which is based upon psychoanalytic principles which stress the unconscious and subconscious processes which can influence group behaviour.

One of the difficulties with these theories is that they rely on fairly sophisticated concepts and terminology which make them difficult to 'translate'. For example, Foulkes was a traditional Freudian analyst in his use of individual psychoanalysis, who compared the

Table 7

Level	Foulkes' definition	What is involved
Current	'the group is experienced as representing the community . . . and the conductor as leader or authority'	This is sometimes expressed as analogous to the chorus in classical Greek tragedy
Transference	'corresponds to mature object relations'	The group is experienced as a family grouping with the members as siblings and the leader as mother or father figure
Projective	Group relations reflect inner object relations	Internal conflicts of bodily and mental images are 'played out' in the group
Primordial	Primitive cultural and collective images predominate	Group members are heavily influenced by the cultural images which reflect their upbringing

characteristics of individual and group treatment and pioneered what came to be known as analytic group therapy.[15] He considers that groups operate on at least four levels simultaneously (see Table 7).

Unless you have a sophisticated background in Freudian/Jungian theory then you will probably find these ideas fairly opaque and difficult to apply. However, if you think about the groups that you have been a member of, you may well be able to remember a time when a group did not appear to behave rationally and where there was no obvious explanation for the feelings of depression or frustration which members fell into. It was observations like these which stimulated perhaps the most influential theory of group processes based on psychoanalytic principles – the work of Wilfred Bion.

Bion: two groups in action

Bion's original interest in group interaction came from his work in the rehabilitation wing of a military hospital during the Second

World War. Several hundred men were in the hospital at any one time for treatment. They were allowed to organise themselves into groups and set their own objectives. Bion observed that many of the groups did not seem to be getting on with the task of helping themselves. Despite the men's obvious commitment, he noticed that the group members did not always seem to be concentrating on the task and often seemed to be distracted by irrelevant factors. After working with these groups for some time, he moved to the Tavistock Clinic in London to work with therapeutic groups. Again, he noticed that groups seemed to behave for much of the time as if therapy was not their major task. From these observations, he developed the following theory.

Whenever a group is interacting there are always two groups operating simultaneously: the work group and the basic assumption group. The work group refers to those structures and processes which are actually working on the conscious task which the group is dealing with. The basic assumption group operates mainly at an unconscious level and consists of 'those group structures and dynamics that operate when the group has met as if for purposes other than the consciously stated task'.[16] The basic assumption group can be one of three types. Each type acts in a different way as shown in Table 8.

The clue that a group has moved from the work phase to a basic assumption state is that the group is no longer working on the actual task it has set itself but has not engaged in any rational justification for this move. Other indicators of the two different states are given in Table 9.

Can we apply this model outside the context of therapeutic groups

Table 8

Basic assumption type	How the group acts
Dependency (Ba.D)	The group acts as if it has met in order to be directed and protected by a very powerful leader
Fight/flight (Ba.F)	The group acts as if it has met either to fight something or to run away from it
Pairing (Ba.P)	The group acts as if it has come together in supportive, intimate, sexually tinged pairs around an "unborn Messiah", a person, idea or Utopia'[17]

Table 9

Work	Basic assumption
Members are more clearly differentiated and autonomous	Members operate in very 'standardised' and uniform fashion
Members behave in typical ways	Members may do or say things which they would not 'normally' do

which Bion started from? It has certainly been applied to groups at work and in education. For example, in a recent overview of psychoanalytic approaches to group theory, Susan Long[18] describes the essential characteristics of Bion's theory as above and then uses a classroom example. Students may feel anxious about thinking out problems for themselves. On the one hand, they risk failure if they get it wrong; on the other hand, they may turn up something more creative than the teacher's ideas and risk incurring his or her anger and displeasure. One way of resolving this anxiety is to accept the belief that the teacher knows everything. The group lapses into Ba.D and is totally dependent on the teacher.

Viewing group behaviour from this perspective means that we can no longer accept a simple classification of acts which can be decoded according to a reasonably standard set of rules and definitions. The meaning of an act is bound up with the complex psychological motives and history which the individuals bring to it. For example, in the research on actual groups which is a major portion of Long's book, she continually highlights how actions at a particular time relate back to previous incidents in the group's history and how members have a very clear sense of this history which guides their actions. She also interprets specific acts in the light of overall themes which seem to reflect group feelings and attitudes. For example, in the analysis of the early stages of one group,[19] she suggests that there was one major episode – an attack on one member, Al. There were a number of actions in this episode, including another member expressing anger, attempts to get Al to talk, sub-group discussion outside of the group, and group discussion of Al inside the whole group. The underlying process is seen as one of scapegoating but not in relation to explicit or conscious criticisms of Al. According to Long, other group members projected their own anxieties on to Al. Al became identified as the person who was 'holding the group back' and the person that the consultant (Long herself) saw as the 'bad' member of the group. This in turn depended upon the group having certain fantasies about the consultant's beliefs.

This brief summary does not do justice to the very detailed and painstaking analysis offered by Long but we can use it to highlight a major problem with psychoanalytic approaches. The validity of the analysis depends upon several factors:

- the validity of the underlying theory
- the quality of the observation of others' behaviour
- the quality of the observer/analyst's insight into their own behaviours

All of these factors can be questioned. In a nutshell, the problem is that the analyst holds the key to the entire meaning of the interaction. As the analyst also decides which actions count as relevant data, then there is no possibility for alternative interpretation and members cannot challenge the dominant interpretation. This line of criticism is summarised by Mike Robinson who considers possible acts by a group who are led by a trainer using Bion's ideas:

> Since there is no object of truth apart from the group itself, no tests of truth and falsity that can be applied by anyone other than the trainer, then the trainer has to be right. If the group recognises this (and seeks to benefit from the trainer's monopoly of insight) then they are dependent. If they challenge this state of affairs, they are manifesting the fight/flight behaviour of the herd. If they try to set up an independent locus of conversation with its own truth values, they are pairing.[20]

In other words, the group cannot 'escape' from the trainer's interpretation and they are stuck in a Catch-22 situation. Only when they accept the trainer's interpretation will they be seen as a mature work group.

So how can we sensibly interpret behaviour in groups?

The message from this chapter so far may come across as somewhat gloomy. If there are all these potential problems and difficulties in observing group interaction then perhaps it has no practical value. That is exactly opposite to the message which I do wish to promote – we must analyse what happens in groups as carefully as possible but we must also be fully aware of the dangers and pitfalls.

This is an issue which I return to in the final chapter of this book. For the moment, I shall suggest some main points to bear in mind when observing group interaction which arise from issues discussed in this chapter:

Observation should have a focus and a purpose

Applying a general category scheme like Bales may be useful in suggesting very broad generalisations but is unlikely to capture the most critical aspects of a given situation. We should use an observation scheme which focuses on the most important characteristics of the situation.

We must clarify the basis on which we make our observations

The definition of what counts as an 'act' or 'episode' is critical, both in terms of establishing that the observations are valid and to check the interpretations.

We cannot ignore group members' history (both in and out of the group)

In everyday groups, the meaning of actions will relate to what has happened before between the group members. Only in some short-term experimental groups can we afford the luxury of ignoring previous histories.

We must include both verbal and nonverbal behaviour

Given what we now know about the scope and impact of nonverbal behaviour, we can no longer rely on verbal transcripts to give us the full picture of group interaction.

We must take into account the feelings and anxieties of group members

Group interaction includes both task and emotional dimensions. We must be able to identify the emotional currents of group life.

We should take account of group members' interpretations of events

Given the ambiguities of behaviour, we must recognise that within the group there are likely to be multiple interpretations of what is going on. These multiple interpretations will affect different members' actions in different ways and this needs to be remembered.

Notes

1 Bales's system was first described in his 1950 book. You will find second-hand accounts of it in virtually any comprehensive social psychology textbook. He developed it and made minor revisions which are explained in his 1970 book. His later system, SYMLOG, is detailed in his 1980 book: Bales, R. F. (1950) *Interaction Process Analysis*. Reading, Massachusetts: Addison-Wesley; Bales, R. F. (1970) *Personality and Interpersonal Behaviour*. New York: Holt, Rinehart and Winston; Bales, R. F., Cohen, S. P. and Williamson, S. A. (1980) *SYMLOG: A system for the multiple level observation of groups*. New York: Free Press.

2 This quote is from page 35 of Brown's book which is one of the few general texts to pay any attention to Bales' later development of IPA. See pages 33–41 of: Brown, R. (1993) *Group Processes. Dynamics within and between groups*. Oxford: Blackwell.

3 See Chapter 8 of: Hartley, P. (1993) *Interpersonal Communication*. London: Routledge.

4 The research I was involved in is described in the unpublished M.Phil. dissertation by Rose Woodhill, Sheffield Hallam University. The study of medical case conferences was undertaken by Luk and Garrud, from the psychiatry department at Queen's Medical Centre in Nottingham: Luk, A. and Garrud, P. (1995) Case conferences – who does what? Paper presented to the Annual Conference of the Special Group in Health Psychology.

5 See note 4.

6 See note 1.

7 This quote is from page 224 of Danziger's book which also contains his observation system. This is well worth studying as an example of how a category system can be developed from first principles and then applied to test significant issues in interpersonal communication: Danziger, K. (1976) *Interpersonal Communication*. Oxford: Pergamon.

8 See note 7.

9 You will find Heron's system described in detail in his own publications. My summary is based on a review by Jaques, pages 24ff. You will also find some suggestions for the practical application of these categories in Chapter 7 of Jaques' book: Heron, J. (1976) *Six-Category Intervention Analysis*. University of Surrey: Human Potential Research Project; Heron, J. (1989) *The Facilitator's Handbook*. London: Kogan Page; Jaques, D. (1991) *Learning in Groups*. 2nd edn. London: Kogan Page.

10 This is fully described in the appendix to Danziger's 1976 book (note 7).

11 Quote taken from page 193 of Danziger's 1976 book (note 7).

12 These functions are described in more detail, page 194ff., in Danziger's 1976 book (note 7).

13 See note 9.

14 For a very useful history of group research and a survey of methods including observation schemes, see Chapters 10 and 11 of: Wheelan, S. (1994) *Group Process. A developmental perspective*. Boston: Alyn & Bacon.

15 Foulkes' approach is explained in the following text. This is very difficult reading if you are not thoroughly versed in psychoanalytic methods and concepts. The book by Long (note 17 below) is more accessible but still pretty complex: Foulkes, S. H. (1964) *Therapeutic Group Analysis*. New York: International Universities Press.

16 There are numerous secondhand accounts of Bion's concepts. His original text is extremely difficult to follow unless you have a sophisticated knowlege of psychoanalytic approaches: Bion, W. R. (1961) *Experiences in Groups*. New York: Basic Books.

17 This quote is taken from an article by Shambaugh which is referred to more extensively in Chapter 4.

18 As well as summarising major psychoanalytic approaches, about half of Long's book is a major case study of a study group which she analysed over a period of time. This analysis shows how she interpreted the members' actions and the group development in considerable detail: Long, S. (1992) *A Structural Analysis of Small Groups*. London: Routledge.

19 See Chapter 11 of Long's book.

20 Robinson's book provides not only a very different approach to group analysis based on systems theory but also an extended analysis of the development of 'real' group interaction, the Brighton Rents Project, quote from page 14: Robinson, M. (1984) *Groups*. London: John Wiley.

Part II

Chapter 4

How do groups change and develop?

This chapter examines whether groups go through any regular or predictable changes or whether group development is much more haphazard and/or accidental. We also explore the practical implications of research in this area, i.e. members and group leaders can use this research to decide how to help their groups change in positive ways.

After identifying important questions and issues, the chapter reviews four different types of theories of group development:

- that groups go through a sequence of stages in a specific order
- that groups go through a sequence of stages but their order may vary
- that groups alternate between different states
- that groups change their central focus as they develop

After looking at some attempts to integrate these views, the chapter brings out the practical implications of these different theories and introduces the concept of planned team development.

What are the important questions?

Consider a group that you have been a member of for a period of time. Think back to when the group first met. What were those first meetings like? What changes have occurred if you compare these early meetings with the group as it exists today? Compare the way that the group members approached both the task and each other at different times in the group's history – did it feel as though the group was progressing through a 'life-cycle'? Is it possible to develop a theory which explains the way that groups change over time? Or are different groups so different that you cannot arrive at any generalisation which is worthwhile? These questions cover some of the main issues which have been investigated by researchers interested in developing theories of group development.

So this chapter focuses on these questions: Do groups change over time? Do groups have a specific life cycle? In what ways do groups change over time? How can you discriminate between different stages or phases of group development? What are the practical implications of these changes?

The following sections explain four major approaches to group development. The best way of getting to grips with these ideas and concepts is to:

- select a group that you have been a member of for some considerable time
- take a few minutes to jot down how you think the group has changed since you joined and how you felt at different stages in its history
- apply each of the theories to that group and see if the theory reflects what you experienced
- if you find that the theory does not predict your experience, consider whether you can account for this difference

After outlining the different approaches, I will raise some of the complications that have been uncovered, including evidence from some studies that suggest that some groups do not experience many real changes at all.

Stages in a definite sequence: forming, storming, norming and performing

The most widely quoted model of group development is the one first suggested by Tuckman in 1965.[1] He surveyed all the studies of small group development he could find and suggested that there was a common pattern – small groups go through the following stages in the following order:

- Forming: a period of uncertainty and confusion
- Storming: a period of conflict about the task and hostility between members
- Norming: the period where group cohesion emerges along with consensus about the task

- Performing: the period where the group can achieve successful performance

This sequence is now often quoted as the 'natural' or typical sequence for all small groups – 'Groups go through certain stages of development'.[2] This is confidently asserted despite the fact that Tuckman identified several important limitations in the literature he surveyed. He noted that it was not truly representative as certain types of groups had been over-represented, especially therapy groups and training groups. Certain other groups were badly under-represented, primarily groups from 'natural' everyday settings. He was also concerned about the validity of the observational methods used in some of the studies he surveyed. Despite these problems, he felt that his description of the stages was a fair synthesis of the studies up to that time. Tuckman's own labels for the different sub-stages are given in italic (see Table 10).

He also made some important comments on these stages which are sometimes 'lost' in later second-hand accounts of his work. For example, he noted that the 'emotional response to task demands', the second stage of task activity, 'will be most evident when the task has as its goal self-understanding and self-change . . . and will be considerably less visible in groups working on impersonal, intellectual tasks'.[3] In other words, this response is much more characteristic of therapy and training groups than of problem-solving groups.

If you take a representative sample of books in areas such as organisational behaviour, training and personal development, you will find that this study has become accepted as the standard formulation of group development. It also highlights a number of practical issues which we shall return to later in this chapter, including the importance of establishing clear group goals and personal relationships to minimise the initial stages of uncertainty, and the possible effects of group conflict.

Tuckman returned to the topic in 1977 and decided that this model could still account for all the studies he could identify.[4] However, he did add a final fifth stage – adjourning. In this final stage, group members know that the group is about to part or split up. They make efforts to complete the task and also say farewells to the other members.

One practical example of this final stage is the group of people on holiday who make friends. The final day of the holiday may well be spent in reassuring the other members that everyone will keep in

Table 10

Stage	Content	Process
Forming	*'orientation to the task'* Members try to identify the task and how they should tackle it. The group decide what information they need and how they are going to get it. Members try to work out the 'ground-rules'.	*'testing and dependence'* Members try to work out 'what interpersonal behaviours are acceptable in the group'. Members will be very dependent on the leader and the reactions of other members.
Storming	*'emotional response to task demands'* This emotionality is 'a form of resistance to the demands of the task on the individual'.	*'intragroup conflict'* 'The lack of unity is an outstanding feature of this phase'. Members are hostile to the leader and to other members.
Norming	*'open exchange of relevant interpretations'* In a therapy or training group, this will mean open discussion of each other's characteristics and behaviour; in a problem-solving group, this will mean open discussion of opinions about the task.	*'development of group cohesion'* Group members start to accept each other and group norms will develop. There will be an emphasis on harmony and conflict or argument will be avoided.
Performing	*'emergence of solutions'* The stage is characterised by 'constructive attempts at successful task completion'.	*'functional role-relatedness'* Group members take on roles which enable them to complete the task.

touch and that the bonds of friendship will survive past the holiday period. The members may be very sincere about this but normally this is simply a ritual – nobody makes serious efforts to contact the other group members after the holiday is over. Most textbook authors do not seem to have read this later article and stay with the four phases!

There is obviously support for this model in the studies that Tuckman surveyed. It also seems to make sense from our everyday experience. We often find that groups go through a period of uncertainty at the very beginning. Members are not sure about how they should relate to the other people and are often unclear about the jobs or tasks which are required. There is often a period of conflict where members with different views try to get their own view established. However, can we simply agree that Tuckman's theory provides a full answer? Before I return to this question, we need to examine other stage theories, and also theories which are based on the idea that groups switch between states rather than follow an orderly sequence.

Group socialisation

Moreland and Levine's model is more of an account of how individual members pass through a group but you will see that the issues involved are very clearly related to issues identified by Tuckman.[5] Focusing upon the way that members are socialised by the group, they identify three fundamental processes:

Evaluation

Individuals continally evaluate whether membership of the group is satisfying their needs; the group is continually evaluating each individual member to see if that individual is making the expected contribution to the group. If a member is not living up to expectations, this will invite disapproval and pressures to change from other members.

Commitment

These evaluations obviously effect the commitment of individuals to the group and vice versa. If there is any imbalance in this commitment then the situation will become unstable.

Role transition

Individuals will move from the status of non-member to new member to full member more or less smoothly depending on their level of commitment. They can also drift away from the group, become marginal and leave.

Over time

Based upon these processes, they identify the five distinct stages described in Table 11.

One aspect of this model which is not strongly highlighted in some others is the emphasis on role transitions and how they are often associated with ritual events.

Welcoming new members: explaining initiation rites

Many groups in society 'welcome' new members by some ritual or ceremony. The most dramatic examples of these ceremonies tend to come from long-established organisations with a strong sense of tradition. These rituals can have a number of predictable conse-

Table 11

Stage	What happens
Investigation	Group recruits or tries to recruit. Prospective members involved in 'sizing up' the group. If successful, this may lead to a formal initiation rite.
Socialisation	New members are socialised into the ways of the group and may also try to influence the group to adjust to their views. Acceptance of the new members depends on the success of this stage.
Maintenance	Members negotiate their roles. A member who is dissatisfied with their role may start to diverge at this stage. This may be accepted in certain groups depending on the norms.
Resocialisation	The group will try to resocialise a member who has diverged beyond accepted limits. If this is not succcessful then the individual will leave or be forced out of the group.
Remembrance	This is the reminiscence stage where both group and individual remember when . . . .

quences for members. Their symbolic function can emphasise the group's self-esteem and distinctiveness, both for new and existing members. They may also be part of the apprenticeship which a group demands of new members and act as a mechanism for eliciting and enhancing group loyalty.

If formal group initiation can have such positive advantages, why do many groups have rituals which are either embarrassing or painful to new recruits? An example of a humiliating or embarrassing ritual would be the welcoming practices of some North American college fraternities. The painful end of the scale would be the methods used by some military groups. Group members may justify these methods in terms of the group's self-image – 'we're tough so you gotta be too' – or in terms of a test for new members – 'if we're all tough, you gotta prove it'. Whatever the rationalisation from the group, there is research evidence that even very negative procedures do have a positive impact on members by increasing their feelings of loyalty to the group assuming they have survived whatever ritual they had to confront.[6]

This impact on group loyalty has been explained in terms of our desire to reduce any inconsistencies when we reflect upon our actions and feelings. On the one hand we have had a miserable experience in the group (the initiation ceremony); on the other hand, we regard membership of the group as attractive or valuable. One way of resolving this inconsistency is to convince ourselves that the group is so important and attractive that it really was worth it to go through all that pain/humiliation.

Of course, this is *not* an argument that groups should use or invent tough initiation procedures to increase membership loyalty. There are both ethical and practical counter-arguments. You cannot justify these procedures from an ethical point of view. From a practical point of view, they may actively discourage prospective members who resent these sometimes bizarre practices.

Stages in sequence but not always this one

There are a number of stage theories which offer variations on the themes set out by Tuckman[7] but which specifically suggest that stages can occur in various different sequences. Among the most interesting are two earlier models by Bennis and Shepard,[8] and by Parsons,[9] and work on decision-making by Bales and Strodtbeck.[10]

Bennis and Shepard

In the early 1950s, Bennis and Shepard developed a theory of group development,[11] mainly on the basis of their observation of T-groups, a form of self-development group which we review in Chapter 12. As a result, we can query whether this model can automatically generalise to other types of group. It has certainly been accepted as an adequate characterisation of many types of training groups.

They propose two major phases with three sub-phases in each. In the first major phase, the group concentrates on issues of authority and structure; in the second phase, the group is most concerned with issues of intimacy and interdependence. This is broadly similar to Tuckman's model except that they suggest that you will find a second phase of hostility between the 'norming' and 'performing' stages. They also emphasise the changing role of the leader in ways similar to the changing centrality model discussed below.

They did not propose that all groups automatically went through the sub-phases that they identified. For example, a group could get stuck in one of the conflict stages and fail to develop any further. Similarly, groups could be forced back to a previous stage.

Parsons

Parson's model was initially based on both task and study groups and has subsequently applied to a wide variety of groups. He identified four major stages in groups, as listed in Table 12. In his

Table 12

Stage	What happens
Latent pattern maintenance (L)	This is the period when stability develops: norms are developed and maintained.
Adaptation (A)	This is the period during which the group structure and roles are worked out.
Goal attainment (G)	This is the period during which the group works to achieve its goal.
Integration (I)	This is the period in which the group structures have to adjust to make sure that the whole group is working effectively.

own work, Parsons suggested[12] that task groups followed a AGIL sequence. In a way this mirrors the ideas of Bales covered below – that, after a focus on the task, the group will need to move to socio-emotional concerns. In contrast, Parsons observed that therapy or learning groups would go through a LIGA sequence. In some later research, Hare[13] suggested that most groups will go through LAIG, although A and I could be reversed. This is not far away from Tuckman, suggesting that the members work through issues of norms and structure before getting down to the task. As an example of how this sort of analysis can help us understand important events, Hare applied this model to the summit conference held at Camp David in 1978 hosted by the American President Jimmy Carter which led to a peace treaty between Egypt and Israel.[14] The group went through the LAIG stages and Hare notes how this development was facilitated by the organisers.

Bales and Strodtbeck

In their investigation of problem-solving groups, they noticed that nearly all the groups followed a sequence of three stages: orientation, evaluation and control, which they went on to recommend as a logical approach to problem-solving. This sequence was also observed in later work.[15]

Recurring phase 1: flipping from task to maintenance

The IPA scheme developed by Bales for observing and classifying group interaction was introduced in Chapter 3. Using this scheme to observe problem-solving groups, he noticed that groups typically switched between concentrating on the task and concentrating on their social and emotional needs – the maintenance of the group. He developed this into an equilibrium theory which proposes that groups need to find a balance between these two areas in order to work effectively over a long period.

This search for equilibrium leads to the group flipping backwards and forwards from one phase to another. If it stays too long in one phase it risks disintegration and collapse. For example:

- if the group concentrates on the task, then . . .
- this will lead to centralised leadership, inequality of contributions and status, and specialisation of roles by the members, and . . .

- this will lead to interpersonal hostility and a breakdown of social cohesion which will move the group to concentrate on group maintenance.

The process will also work the other way:

- if the group concentrates on group maintenance, then . . .
- this will lead to diffuse leadership, equality of contributions and status, and lack of specialisation of roles by the members, and . . .
- this will lead to the group becoming 'inefficient' and losing control of the task which will move the group to concentrate on the task again, and . . .
- we are back where we started and the cycle continues.

Recurring phase 2: flipping from work to anxiety

A very different approach comes from the work of Bion, also introduced in Chapter 3. The change here is between the work group and one or more varieties of the basic assumption group. The task of the leader according to this theory is to accurately diagnose the presence of a basic assumption phase and take action to move the group into the work group mentality.

Changing centrality: remember that leader, whatsisname . . .

This model also derives from psychoanalytic principles and follows from the early conceptualisation of the role of the leader by Sigmund Freud.[16] Freud suggested that the relationship between group members and their leader was based upon a process of identification, a critical concept within psychoanalysis. Through this process, the member's own ego-ideal is replaced by the leader and this forges a relationship he equated with others such as the hypnotist–subject relationship. The fact that all the members go through this process provides the tie that binds the group together.

The notion of group development which follows from this theory involves the decreasing centrality of the leader and the corresponding rise of the group culture.

Are you sure groups change?

There have been attempts to discover situations where groups do not seem to go through any developmental sequences. Cissna reviewed the negative evidence and found it 'not . . . persuasive'.[17] Rather than waste energy looking for negative examples, he urged researchers to concentrate more on 'identifying significant differences and similarities in group development among various groups'.

This leads us to recent attempts to synthesise the models discussed so far in this chapter. I have selected three for specific attention as they offer different solutions to the issues of change:

- work by Philip Shambaugh which relates group development to two underlying dimensions[18]
- work by Susan Wheelan which includes a reworking of Tuckman plus a scheme for observation and diagnosis plus practical guidance[19]
- a recurring 'life-cycle' model from Steve Worchel[20]

Underlying dimensions

Philip Shambaugh[21] suggests that development involves movement along two related dimensions: the psychological closeness of the group members, and the accumulation of group culture. As far as psychological closeness is concerned, members will oscillate between feelings of warmth and closeness and feelings of hostility and competitiveness. Over time these fluctuations will become less marked as the members become more comfortable and trusting with one another. Shambaugh defines group culture as 'the mainly implicit, internalised totality of group-relevant points of view, understandings, practices and norms' and sees it developing step by step with periods of growth interspersed with plateaux of no change. He argues that these two movements incorporate the ideas of Tuckman, Bales and Bion into the 'fluctuating, stepwise course' of group development. However, his underlying model does seem very dependent upon processes which are characteristic of therapy and training groups. As with Tuckman, there is the problem of extending this analysis to groups in broader contexts.

On from Tuckman

At first sight, the model proposed by Wheelan looks like another slight reworking of Tuckman.[22] There are five stages which come in a definite and logical order: 'some processes or stages occur before others in group development. Dependency is less likely to occur

Table 13

Stage	What happens
Dependency and inclusion	Members are very reliant on the leader. Communication very tentative and polite. Members are anxious and fearful. Members shy away from the task.
Counterdependency and flight	Conflict either between leader and member(s) or between members. Members continue to shy away from the task. Individuals try to work out their roles.
Trust and structure	Conflict is successfully resolved. Norms and rules can now be decided. More open communication. Fewer power struggles. Members feel more secure.
Work	Group works effectively.
Termination	The group disbands having completed the task.

after trust and structure are established, for example.'[23] These are described in Table 13. However, she also accepts that this order can fluctuate as groups can get 'stuck' or regress to a previous stage. In her examples of 'stuckness', she notes that some groups can remain dependent for long periods of time. As a result the group is unable to function without the leader present and is also unable to get involved in any collaborative or thoughtful work. Another example is the group which gets stuck in a conflict phase and self-destructs.

Apart from her research work to test and validate this model, there are three other important contributions in Wheelan's work: specific criteria to identify each stage, the development of an observation system to test the model, and her practical advice to members and leaders.

Criteria

One difficulty with all stage models is determining the transition point for one stage to another. Wheelan supplies a comprehensive list of criteria against each stage. For example, stage one has twenty-one criteria including 'Member compliance is high' and 'The leader is seen as benevolent and competent.' Stage four has forty criteria including 'Members are clear about their roles' and 'The group chooses participatory decision-making methods.'

Observation system

Wheelan uses a seven category observation system, designed to categorise each and every 'verbal unit' in ways which enable her to test the model. For example, one category is dependency, 'which shows the inclination to conform with the dominant mood of the group, to follow suggestions made by the leader, and generally, to demonstrate a desire for direction from others', as in 'I don't know what to do'.[24] If her model is correct, dependent statements will be highest during the first two stages.

Practical advice

Associated with each stage of the model, she provides practical advice for members and leaders of different types of groups. Table 14 summarises critical advice for leaders and members of work groups at each stage. One important point here is that *both* leader and members are responsible for helping the group develop.

Here we go round again

Worchel[25] also claims to offer a model which can be applied to all groups and which shows the ebb and flow of group life. He claims that the model integrates previous work and offers it for further testing and development. He suggests six phases which are then repeated for as long as the group remains in existence (see Table 15).

This last model certainly relates to experiences I have had with groups which have been organised round a theme such as fund-raising where there is a continual need to develop new projects and where there is always a continual struggle to keep both old and new members on board and actively involved.

Table 14

Stage	What leaders need to do	What members need to do
Dependency and inclusion	Enable open discussion of values, goals, tasks and leadership.	Request information about goals. Raise their personal concerns.
Counter-dependency and flight	Make sure that the conflicting issues are dealt with constructively.	Work to resolve conflicts constructively.
Trust and structure	Organise in ways that make the group productive.	Organise in ways that make the group productive.
Work	Periodically assess how the group is going to ensure that the group can adjust to any changes.	Periodically assess how the group is going to ensure that the group can adjust to any changes.

Table 15

Stage	What happens
Discontent	Members feel withdrawn and helpless.
Precipitating event	Some event occurs which expresses the dissatisfaction and which members see as establishing some common ground.
Group identification	Members focus on defining the group in terms of who is now a member.
Group productivity	Goals are identified and planning takes place.
Individuation	Individuals tend to return to focusing on their own needs.
Decay	Members become preoccupied with their own needs at the expense of collaboration.
And then back to discontent and here we go again	

But chaos may still be lurking

Despite Susan Wheelan's claim that research which argues against the notion of group development is 'minimal', and despite Cissna's review which suggests that previous research is flawed, we can still find studies which suggest that chaos and disruption may be more prevalent than some of the models imply. For example, Poole and Roth[26] studied 47 recorded decisons made by a total of 29 groups, including a mixture of real decision-making teams and experimental groups. He found that only eleven followed the orderly sequence identified by Bales and Strodtbeck earlier in this chapter. Most groups engaged in some recycling – shifting back and forward between stages – or what he termed 'conflict breakpoints' where groups came to a dead end and had to refocus themselves. One common finding was that many groups started by immediately adopting a likely solution. They then concentrated on debating this before really working out the full implications of the problem. This is a common pattern in groups on training exercises, especially when the groups are anxious to succeed and there are time pressures involved.

Making use of this research: the notion of planned team development

Unfortunately I have to repeat the point that we have insufficient research on everyday groups to decide how far we can generalise some of these theories. However, we can suggest that some form of development is likely and adopt the practice of diagnosing the likely stages and then intervening appropriately as illustrated in the discussion of Susan Wheelan's model above. This leads us to the concept of planned team development.

Planned team development

One of the consequences of the increasing use of teams in organisations is the increased emphasis on ways of getting groups to work together more effectively. This is discussed in more detail in Chapter 10. Here I shall introduce a few examples to show how the idea of planned team development can build upon some of the ideas which have come out of the research on group development.

Manuals on 'how to develop your team' are typically built around two main principles.

Diagnosing the group stage

There are many ways of diagnosing the present state of team interaction. For example, you can apply a model like Tuckman's to see if the group exhibits the characteristics he associated with the performing stage. This is the approach used in a typical team-building manual by Hardingham and Royal.[27] For a rough and ready guide, try the following checklist adapted from this manual and organised as an acronym of PERFORM (see Table 16).

Of course, you would not expect straightforward 'yes/no' answers to all these questions and you can envisage a scale on each of these factors from very high to very low. Their more detailed diagnostic questionnaire uses such a scale.[28]

Intervening to 'move the group on'

Effective diagnosis leads to action. For example, a group which seems to be moving into Tuckman's storming phase could be diverted from unnecessary conflict if the aims and objectives of the members could be openly discussed. In other words, a skilful

Table 16

Characteristic	Critical question	Common indicator of problems
Productivity	Is the group doing enough?	Ill-tempered boss.
Empathy	Do members feel comfortable with each other?	Tense atmosphere at meetings.
Roles and goals	Do members know what is required of them?	Confusion about priorities.
Flexibility	Are members open to outside influence and contributions?	Complaints from outside.
Openness	Does everyone say what they really think?	Lack of debate.
Recognition	Do members praise each other and publicise achievement?	Backbiting and sarcasm.
Morale	Do people want to be in this team?	Where did everybody go?

chair could move the group on to norming. Another example would be an intervention designed to move the group quickly through the initial forming stage by using an appropriate ice-breaking exercise.

Other intervention strategies will be discussed when we return to this topic in Chapter 10.

Notes

1 The two critical articles by Tuckman are listed below. It is well worth reading the 1965 article and contrasting it with later accounts (including mine) which often give a much more 'dogmatic' account of the stages and their likely occurrence. The quotes are from his 1965 article: Tuckman, B. W. (1965) Developmental sequence in small groups, *Psychological Bulletin*, 63, 384–99; Tuckman, B. W. and Jensen, M. A. (1977) Stages in small group development revisited, *Group and Organizational Studies*, 2, 419–27.

2 This quote is fairly typical of the conclusions reached in texts on organisation behaviour – it is from page 314 of the popular text by Tosi *et al.* Unlike some other texts, they do add the cautionary note that 'all group stages do not always occur' (page 316, quoting the article by Gersick) but do not go into further detail on how or why these differences occur: Tosi, H. L., Rizzo, J. R., and Carroll, S. J. (1994) *Managing Organizational Behaviour*. 3rd edn. London: Blackwell; Gersick, C. J. G. (1989) Making time: transitions in task groups. *Academy of Management Journal*, 3, 274–309.

3 See note 1.

4 See note 1.

5 See Moreland and Levine's text for a fuller description of these processes: Moreland, R. L. and Levine, J. M. (1994) *Understanding Small Groups*. Boston, MA: Allyn and Bacon.

6 See Brown p. 23ff. for further discussion of the psychological process underpinning initiation rites: Brown, R. (1988) *Group Processes. Dynamics within and between groups*. Oxford: Blackwell.

7 You can find a chart comparing thirteen models of group development on pages 38–9 of: Jaques, D. (1991) *Learning in Groups*. 2nd edn. London: Kogan Page.

8 The original article by Bennis and Shepard dates back to the 1950s. Bennis, W. G. and Shepard, H. A. (1956) A theory of group development. *Human Relations*, 9, 415–37.

9 See: Parsons, T., Bales, R. F. and Shils, E. A. (1953) *Working Papers in the Theory of Action*. Glencoe, IL: Free Press.

10 This study was part of Bales' early work following the development of IPA: Bales, R. F. and Strodtbeck, F. L. (1951) Phases in group problem-solving. *Journal of Abnormal and Social Psychology*, 46, 485–95.

11 See note 8.

12 See note 9.

13 For an example of practical analysis, see: Hare, A. P. (1967) Small

group development in the relay assembly testroom. *Sociological Inquiry*, 37, 169–82.

14 For the full analysis of this important meeting, see both: Hare, A. P. and Naveh, D. (1984) Group development at Camp David Summit, 1978. *Small Group Behaviour*, 15, 299–318; Hare, A. P. and Naveh, D. (1986) Conformity and creativity: Camp David. *Small Group Behaviour*, 17, 243–68.

15 See note 10.

16 Freud's work on this was first published in 1921 but has been regularly reprinted: Freud, S. (1965) *Group Psychology and the Analysis of the Ego*. New York: Bantam Books.

17 For a review of studies, see Cissna's article: Cissna, K. N. (1984) Phases in group development: the negative evidence. *Small Group Behaviour*, 15, 3–32.

18 See: Shambaugh, P. W. (1978) The development of the small group. *Human Relations*, 31, 283–95.

19 If I had to recommend only one book to read on group development it would be Susan Wheelan's: Wheelan, S. (1994) *Group Process. A developmental perspective*. Boston: Alyn and Bacon.

20 Worchel's article contains a number of interesting comments on the nature of research into small group behaviour as well as his developmental model: Worchel, S. (1994) You can go home again. Returning group research to the group context with an eye on developmental contexts. *Small Group Research*, 25, 205–23.

21 See note 18.

22 See note 19.

23 See page 18 of Wheelan, note 19 above.

24 See page 177 of Wheelan, note 19 above.

25 See note 20.

26 For a detailed description of this study and the methodology, see: Poole, M. S. and Roth, R. A. (1989) Decision development in small groups IV. A typology of group decision paths. *Human Communication Research*, 15, 323–56.

27 Hardingham and Royal are directors of Interactive Skills Limited, a human resources consultancy active in organisational teambuilding. Their book is a practical guide to planned team development with many interesting examples drawn from real organisations: Hardingham, A. and Royal, J. (1994) *Pulling together. Teamwork in practice*. London: Institute of Personnel and Development.

28 See pages 59ff. of Hardingham and Royal, note 27 above.

Chapter 5

How are members influenced by the group?

This chapter outlines important areas and phenomena of social influence which are especially relevant to small group interaction. Starting from well-established research on the nature of conformity and the development of norms, we identify some of the processes which try to explain how people react to pressures from the majority in the group. These processes are then re-examined in terms of other research such as minority influence which seems to offer a conflicting view.

Finally, the chapter suggests ways of applying these ideas in groups to encourage independence and the free flow of communication.

Social influence: an area in need of integration

The study of social influence has been an important topic within social science but has been studied in very different ways and from different perspectives. Recently there have been some valiant attempts to integrate the different approaches but this is by no means complete.[1] This chapter focuses upon how we can explain the pressures that members apply to each other. Influence which is based on more formal power and authority structures is discussed in Chapter 6 where we explore leadership behaviour.

There has been a very strong tradition of research into conformity pressures and the development of norms in groups – shared standards of behaving and thinking which members accept. This has concentrated on the way that a majority in the group will exert pressure on an individual or individuals to come into line with the group expectations. After investigating how this pressure can operate, we compare these findings with an area of research which has investigated influence from the opposite direction – where a minority in the group is successful in convincing the majority to change its ways.

Social conformity – classic studies

We obviously conform to a whole range of social pressures in everyday life, for example in our choice of dress and appearance. But how do these pressures work and have their impact on us? This section starts to answer this question by outlining a few classic studies of social influence, identifying processes which can explain the findings and then relating these processes to everyday groups. For all these studies, I explain the situation first so you can imagine yourself in the subject's position: how would you react? How would you feel? Would your reactions be typical of your peer group?

The classic studies are Muzafer Sherif's study of the autokinetic phenomenon,[2] Solomon Asch's study of the impact of the unanimous majority,[3] Kurt Lewin's work with American housewives,[4] and the studies of bystander intervention by Darley and Latané.[5]

Have you seen the light? – The autokinetic phenomenon

The autokinetic phenomenon is a well-known optical illusion. If you sit in a completely darkened room and there is a tiny stationary point of light visible at the other end of the room, after a while you will see this light move around, unless you have been told about the effect beforehand. Assuming that you see the light move then you will be able to estimate the degree of movement from the original position.

Different people will see the light move to different degrees. Muzafer Sherif knew of this illusion and wanted to use it to see how groups responded to it.[6] So imagine yourself in the following situation:

You have been presented with the illusion individually (but you are not aware that it is an illusion). You have seen the spot of light move and estimate that it moved around 3 feet away from its original position. You have now joined a group of three in the darkened room and been asked to say how much the spot moved. You repeat your estimate of 3 feet. The other two individuals report movements of 1 foot and 2 feet respectively. How does this influence your perception of the situation?

This is repeated a few times. On each occasion you are asked to say how you saw the spot move and you hear the reactions of the other two. Does your reaction change? A few weeks later you are invited back and asked to look at the light again on an individual basis.

Consider your reactions before you read on.

And what happened

Sherif repeated this situation with many groups. In each case, he assessed how individuals reacted to the illusion, and then put them in trios so that all three were aware of the others' reactions. After a few trials he noticed that the group members were starting to agree on the degree of movement. Not only did individuals come to agree on a group norm but this effect lasted when those individuals were later tested on their own; this effect could be long-lasting. In the example above, we would expect your verdict to move towards 2 feet which would become the group norm.

But why should this happen? There was no incentive to agree, the individuals were not known to each other, and they had no intention of meeting again after the experiment. Sherif concluded that the imprtance of others' opinions in this situation was that they acted as a frame of reference, enabling individuals to arrive at a stable and coherent view of the situation, particularly important in an ambiguous situation. But what if you confront people with a completely unambiguous task – how do they then respond to conflicting judgements?

Responding to the unanimous majority

Although this study was originally done back in the very early 1950s, it is still relevant to any discusion of how majority influence and norms operate in groups, and the original accounts of the research are well worth reading.[7] Again, put yourself in the role of subject:

You have volunteered to participate in an experiment on visual perception. When you arrive at the psychology laboratory, you find that you are one of a group of eight subjects who are sat in a line in front of the experimenter who explains that he will show you a card with a single line on it and then a card with 3 lines on it, labelled A, B and C. Your task is to decide which of the 3 lines is the same

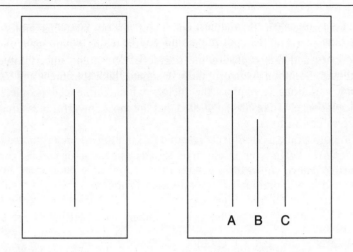

Figure 3

length as the original. Everyone has to give their answers out loud
and you are the last to do so, being at the end of the line. This is
repeated many times with different sets of cards. All seems to go
well the first few times as everyone agrees on the right answer. On
the next occasion the set of cards looks like the ones in Figure 3.
One by one, all of the other subjects gives the answer B. It is now
your turn to answer. You can see quite clearly that the right answer
is A but what do you say? What effect do the other subjects'
answers have on you? Do you feel that maybe you are wrong? Do
you feel that maybe you have misinterpreted the task? Do you feel
that the others are wrong but you are tempted to give the wrong
answer to avoid any embarrassment?

Whatever you decide this first time, you discover that this problem of being in the minority happens regularly as the experiment
proceeds, on 12 times out of the total of 18. Decide how you would
feel and act before you read on.

And the real situation

The study became recognised as the classic demonstration of the
power of the majority on the individual. As you may have guessed
from the account above, the other seven subjects were stooges
working to a predetermined script set by the experimenter. They
give the wrong answer in twelve trials in the experiment. However,

the real subjects in the actual experiment did not spot this subterfuge. They were convinced that the others were giving genuine responses and this caused some degree of stress and uncertainty. Although Solomon Asch originally designed this experiment and its many variations to explore the factors which influenced people's independence, the results suggested that the most powerful pressures were to conform.

So how would 100 subjects respond (all intelligent undergraduate students)? Again you might like to answer these questions for yourself before you read on:

- How many subjects would follow the group and give the wrong answer at least once?
- How many subjects would follow the group and give the wrong answer every time the conflict arose?
- How many subjects would never follow the group, remain independent, and always give the right answer?

Remember that the task is unambiguous – if you ask individuals to do it, they achieve the right answer over 99 per cent of the time. And remember that all the responses are public – the real subject always has to say their answer out loud and always last.

And what happened

Although the results are sometimes represented as demonstrating the overwhelming power of the majority, they also show a mix of conformity and independence:

- the subjects conformed to the stooges on 33 per cent of the critical trials
- twenty-five per cent of the subjects remained totally independent
- twenty-five per cent of the subjects moved towards the group on eight or more trials
- thirty-three per cent of the subjects conformed on 50 per cent or more of the critical trials
- five per cent of the subjects gave in every time
- all subjects showed significant levels of concern and tension, even those who remained resolutely independent
- there were also very different personal reactions to the situation

You may like to compare different textbook accounts of this study. Do they emphasise the fact that 25 per cent of subjects remained independent or that 75 per cent gave in at least once? Does this make you feel more or less cheerful about our capacity to be independent and free-thinking?

So what does this show us? Asch was certainly surprised by the level of conformity he uncovered. He went on to do variations of this original design to decide what factors could encourage subjects to remain independent. One important finding was the influence of public or private commitment – when subjects have to give private answers, conformity drops. Conformity also drops dramatically when one of the stooges gives the correct answer. If you feel you have a 'friend' in the rest of the group, this encourages you to stick with your own opinion. Additional stooges giving correct answers did not have such a dramatic effect. This shows that it is the unanimity of the group rather than the numbers lined up against you which is the critical factor.

Another interesting result was the different reactions by different subjects. Among the subjects who remained independent, there was a variety of reactions, from assertive independence, through rather withdrawn attitudes, to subjects who obviously felt extremely uncomfortable but had to stick with the right answer. Among the yielders, there was a corresponding variety. A small minority claimed that they had simply stated what they saw and denied any influence. Others recognised the difference but rationalised that they must have misunderstood and that the majority had got it right. Some went along cynically, deciding not to risk any ridicule or embarrassment.

What are the underlying processes?

Again we can ask why subjects should have felt the way they did. You could argue that there was no incentive to conform given that the other subjects were strangers and there was no overt pressure from the experimenter to give the conformist answer.

Perhaps the critical observation is that, except for a small minority of subjects, conformity is a matter of degree. It is not all-or-nothing: subjects give in on some but not all trials; if the majority give an extreme response (one that is very clearly wrong like C in Figure 3), many subjects chose the answer that was moderately wrong (like B in Figure 3).

The most common theory used to explain these results is that there are two independent influence processes at work: normative

and informational influence.[8] Normative influence is that influence
to conform which is based upon our motivation to gain social
acceptance from other members of the group – we conform to
others' expectations in order to please them and be accepted as a
member of the group. Informational influence is influence where we
accept the opinions and judgements of others as accurate and
objective evidence of what is really true in the situation. The
accounts of Asch's subjects clearly show that both these processes
were at work to different degrees in different people. But can this be
the complete explanation?

When conformity disappears

Perrin and Spencer carried out a straight replication of Asch using
undergraduate students.[9] They chose students from academic backgrounds in science, mathematics and engineering to be sure that the
subjects would not have heard of the original Asch studies and so
would not have any prior expectations (this was also checked in the
debriefing). The students' reactions to being put in the minority
position were very similar to those reported by Asch – including
confusion, stress, and concern whether they had interpreted the task
correctly. Despite this, they did not yield to conformity. Out of 396
test trials, only one student conformed on one occasion. On the basis
of these results, Perrin and Spencer concluded that the level of
conformity Asch reported was 'a product of the period and culture
within which it was first demonstrated'. They noted that the Asch
studies were originally carried out in the America of the 1950s, then
home of Senator McCarthy and the anti-communist intolerance
which reached almost paranoid proportions. This was not a period
when students were noted for either free-thinking or independent
attitudes.

Needless to say, this experiment aroused considerable interest.
Asch himself wrote to commend it, noting that:

> the McCarthy period produced effects vastly more serious and
> radical than what psychologists could study with their diabolical
> (but fortunately feeble) procedures.[10]

There followed a lively few months in the correspondence pages of
the British psychology journals which suggested that there had been
more replications of Asch than we had been aware of, including

several in British universities.[11] Many of these had found conformity levels similar to Asch.

Perrin and Spencer carried out further permutations of the Asch
experiment on different groups:[12] including young offenders on
probation, and with young unemployed West Indian groups in a
depressed area of London. These groups were in positions where
group loyalty was much more relevant to them and where the
experiment more clearly represented the hierarchical authority relations of their everyday life. In these conditions, conformity reap-
peared to near the levels observed by Asch.

Another study inspired by Perrin and Spencer suggests even
further complications. When the Asch experiment was repeated on
different groups of American and British university students in
1983, there was significant evidence of conformity and no significant difference between the British and American groups.[13] The
level of conformity was less than in the original Asch studies. Could
this have been yet another cultural effect? Between 1980 and 1983
the British experienced the Falklands war – did this increase social
cohesiveness in ways which also affected student groups? We shall
return to these problems of explanation later in this chapter after
completing our round of selected studies.

When 'housewives' talk

The influence of group consensus on individual attitudes was vividly
demonstrated by Kurt Lewin in some work conducted during the
Second World War in the United States.[14] Given the need for
careful consumption to cope with war emergencies, there was a
drive to encourage housewives (and this was at a time when this
description had very different cultural overtones) to increase their
consumption of less 'atttractive' but still nutritional meat products
like kidneys and hearts. Of course, this was well before the value of
vegetarian habits became generally accepted.

Again imagine you are a subject in this study:
You are invited to attend a lecture from a distinguished expert which
shows how important good nutrition is to the war effort and how
buying these different cuts of meat will contribute. Alternatively,
you are invited to participate in a discussion group after being
provided with the relevant information. Your group is asked to
arrive at a consensus decision on how they are going to respond.
In either case, you are asked some time later if your buying and

eating habits have changed in any way. Which method of communicating would have most influence upon your behaviour, and why?

When Lewin investigated the impact of the lectures, he found that they did little to influence the housewives' behaviour, regardless of the quality of the lecturer. However, when groups were given the same information and then asked to discuss the issues and arrive at a consensus about how they should respond, there was a significant impact. Over 30 per cent of the discussion groups changed their food habits in line with their consensus decision whereas only around 3 per cent of the lecture groups were influenced. The effect was repeated in studies advocating different products such as feeding cod liver oil to babies.

Later studies confirmed that the important process here was the reaching of a decision which was shared by the group members, as opposed to just the discussion. Once members became committed to a group decision, they felt obliged to carry it out later, although as the statistics show, only a large minority actually changed their behaviour.

When bystanders bystand

The final research to examine in this section was stimulated by an infamous murder which took place in New York in 1964 – the Kitty Genovese incident. Again, visualise the incident and assess how you would have acted:

You live in an upstairs apartment in a block in a reasonably quiet residential area of New York. About 3.00 a.m. you are woken by the sound of a woman screaming. You get out of bed and look out of your window to the courtyard below. You see a woman who appears to be fighting off an attack by a man who appears to have a knife in his hand. You notice that the man runs away and the woman continues to scream for help. If you continue to look out of the window, you see the man return. There is a further scuffle, more screams from the woman and the man runs off again. A few minutes later, the man returns and carries out a final attack on the woman. He leaves her to bleed to death where she lies in the courtyard.

What would you do? How would you feel? How would you explain your action (or inaction)? Answer these questions before you read on.

Who were the bystanders?

When the police arrived on the scene, they found thirty-eight people who had watched the murder from behind their apartment windows – none had intervened, none had contacted the police. They gave various reasons for their inaction, including fear of being attacked themselves, fear of getting involved with the police, and various rationalisations about the seriousness of the incident – wasn't it just a lovers' quarrel?

The savagery of the attack meant that this murder was extensively reported in the media and this provoked not only a debate about a possible decline in feelings of social conscience and altruism but also some research which was designed to explore people's motives and reactions to crisis situations.

The most famous of these was a series of studies initiated by Bibb Latané and John Darley[15] where they simulated accidents and then studied how individuals reacted, how groups reacted, and how individuals reacted in the presence of stooges who seemed unconcerned. Where individuals were confronted by others who did not react to the situation, they seemed to be thrown into a state of 'social paralysis' and their own reactions to the emergency were either blunted or delayed.

Latané and Darley concluded that most people do not react instinctively or instantaneously to emergencies but have to make a series of (often subconscious) decisions before intervening. These decisions can be summarised as a series of questions:

- Is something going on?
- Is it an emergency?
- Is it my responsibility to get involved?
- What action is appropriate in this situation?
- How can I carry out this action?

A negative answer (or a 'don't know') to any of these questions means you will not move on to the next question and you will not intervene. So failure to respond to an emergency is not a straightforward issue of your personality characteristics – how kind-hearted you are (or not). The process of social comparison, where you review what other people are doing, is a critical part of the process. The status and identity of those others is also very important. One hypothesis which Latané and Darley have tested and confirmed is that, the more people who are bystanders at an emergency, the less likely or more slowly will any one bystander intervene to help. If you feel ill and you are going to faint, try to move to away from a crowded area! You may also wish to consider some of the other generalisations that have come out of research into altruistic behaviour:[16]

- your desire to help may be affected by the mood you are in
- your desire to help will be affected by the identity of the person(s) in distress
- your desire to help will be affected by the likely consequences of getting involved

Moving back to the main topic of this book, the processes which have been highlighted in this research and which are especially relevant are threefold:

- diffusion of responsibility: if other members of a group are around us, we may feel less personally responsible
- social definition of the situation: we look to others' reactions to help us work out what is going on
- social comparison: not only do we look to the reactions of others but we take account of who those others are. We will be more influenced by others who are perceived as similar to ourselves

Factors in social conformity

The studies we have surveyed, along with numerous others which have been conducted over the past few decades, suggest a number of critical factors which will increase or decrease the impact of conformity pressures:[17]

The importance of reference group membership

We are more likely to conform when we feel a strong sense of shared identity with other group members who are perceived as exerting pressure on us.

Consensual validation and social support

We do compare our reactions and responses with others' reactions and the level of social support we receive is important as a reinforcer of what we have decided. Confronting a unanimous majority will create the most pressure to change.

Surveillance and public compliance

There is a very big difference between providing a public and private statement of your opinion. Linked to this is the amount of surveillance – how are your reactions being monitored by the rest of the group? This factor is also very important in the analysis of power and authority which follows in Chapter 6.

Stimulus ambiguity and subjective uncertainty

The more ambiguous the stimulus, the more uncertain you are likely to be, and the more influence other opinions may have on you.

Extremity of the norm

When we are confronted with a dramatic difference of opinion between our opinion and the group majority we may 'compromise' and move to an intermediate position.

Minority influence: the other side of the coin?

Serge Moscovici had become interested during the 1960s in how innovation occurred in science.[18] This often seemed to come from groups who were on the fringe or even marginal to the scientific field in question. They developed a dissenting voice which challenged the scientific orthodoxy of the day. Moscovici developed ideas about innovation and how new ideas tended to emerge not so much out of perceived errors in the conventional thinking but because a 'surplus' knowledge developed. There were so many findings to explain that a group was able to develop new ideas which did not depend on the dominant approaches. But how did this dissenting voice come to be accepted and replace the previous orthodoxy? Conventional research in social conformity had no real explanation for this, thanks to the overwhelming attention given to majority pressures in the research literature.

From discussion of how influential new thinkers had achieved an impact, he developed hypotheses on which factors were critical and tested them out in a series of ingenious experiments. In brief, he argues that minority influence will be successful to the extent that the minority adopts a specific behavioural style.

The most important characteristic of this style is consistency and there are two aspects to this. Not only must the minority members agree among themselves but they must also maintain this opinion over time. It is also important to emphasise that this consistency must be recognised by the other members of the group. Other influential features of the successful behavioural style include:

- investment: the minority will be more likely to be successful if the other members recognise that they have invested a lot of time and energy in their cause, perhaps also making significant personal sacrifices.
- autonomy: the minority is seen as acting as a result of genuinely held principles and not out of vested interests or from ulterior motives.
- open-minded and reasonable: the minority is neither too rigid nor too flexible.

One interesting aside is that this line of research was intially taken up by a group of European researchers who perhaps shared 'a self-conception as an "outsider"' and were motivated to develop the ideas in opposition to a dominant view which tended to 'view dissidence in perjorative terms'.[19]

The underlying processes

Two major theories have been suggested to explain these findings:

Conversion theory

This is Moscovici's own explanation where he attempts to suggest processes which can cover both majority and minority influence. He argues that, in majority influence, individuals will focus on the majority's message and fail to pay attention to any alternative views. As a result the message will be accepted but not analysed in any way and there will be public compliance. However, when a minority dissents, this forces individuals to focus on their own responses and judgements in order to understand how the minority could possibly see things that way. Although individuals are not likely to admit publicly that they might agree with the majority, this re-examination of their position can lead to a private opinion change which will start the ball rolling towards the minority view.

This theory can be used to generate predictions. For example, if a minority view is expressed, this theory predicts that this will set off a validation process where individuals analyse what the minority says and generate arguments for and against it.

Different thinking styles

In contrast, Nemeth has argued that majority and minority influence are both governed by cognitive processes based on different thinking styles.[20] Majority influence leads to convergent thinking which again leads to the neglect of alternatives. Minority influence leads to divergent thinking and the consideration of creative alternative processes.

This leads to different predictions from Moscovici's explanation. For example, the response to a minority view will not just trigger more arguments but will induce divergent thinking which will lead to a much wider range of issues being discussed.

Comparisons and conclusions

There are now a number of studies which directly compare predictions from these two theories.[21] One important recent example 'planted' minority influence agents in real workgroups and observed their impact, and also how they felt in the role.[22] This study supported Nemeth's model and found that the agent's presence led to much more divergent thinking and more original solutions. This was achieved without any more conflict than in the comparison groups which reinforces the general conclusion that minority influence does not necessarily mean an increase in conflict. The agents did experience some stress and this was especially marked when the agent was in a 'double minority'. This is where the person was not only expressing different opinions but also in a different social category to the majority of the group, e.g. the black woman in a mainly white group.

The other important conclusion which arises from this research is the number of positive benefits which can result from acts of minority influence:

Minority influence can prevent excessive conformity by providing a model of dissenting behaviour which bolsters the courage of other group members to speak up.[23]

Using this research in practical situations

There are a number of practical steps which groups can adopt if they want to avoid some of the negative effects of the processes discussed in this chapter:

Encourage the minority and especially any 'double minorities'

The group can behave in line with values and attitudes which can either support or hamper the expression of minority opinion. It may be especially stressful for individuals who find themselves in a double minority position and this calls for appropriate sensitivity from the other individuals in the group.

Treat agreement with suspicion

What seems to be unanimous agreement may disguise a silent minority. Group members can question whether agreement is really valid by acting as devil's advocate and pitching in a contrary view.

Support the expression of opinion

Group members are all responsible for the way they react to others' suggestions. These reactions will either encourage or discourage the expression of contrary opinions.

Explore alternatives

There are all sorts of ways in which groups can actively explore alternative methods of approaching a problem which can encourage minority opinions. Many of these points will be revisited in Chapter 8 where we look at the processes of group problem-solving and decision-making.

Notes

1 The integrative text which is most relevant to the concerns of this book is by John Turner: Turner, J. C. (1991) *Social Influence*. Milton Keynes: Open University Press.

2 Although Sherif's book is now over 60 years old, the issues it addresses are still very much alive. His later textbook is also still well worth reading: Sherif, M. (1936) *The Psychology of Social Norms*. New York: Harper and Brothers; Sherif, M. and Sherif, C. W. (1969) *Social Psychology*. New York: Harper and Row.

3 Asch originally published his results in 1951. His research monograph is still well worth chasing out for the detailed descriptions of subject's reactions: Asch, S. E. (1951) Effects of group pressure upon the modification and distortion of judgement. In Guetzkow, G. (ed.) *Groups, Leadership and Men*. Pittsburgh: Carnegie Press; Asch, S. E. (1956) Studies of independence and conformity. A minority of one against a unanimous majority. *Psychological Monographs*, 60, no. 9 (whole no. 416).

4 The original studies are described and discussed in: Lewin, K. (1947) Group decision and social change. In Newcomb, T. M. and Hartley, E. L. (eds) *Readings in Social Psychology*. New York: Holt, Rinehart and Winston, 330–44.

5 The major article which sparked off a number of investigations was: Darley, J. M. and Latané, B. (1968) Bystander intervention in emergencies: Diffusion of responsibility. *Journal of Personality and Social Psychology*, 8, 377–83.

6 See note 2.

7 See note 3.

8 This theory was outlined in the 1955 paper by Deutsch and Gerard: Deutsch, M. and Gerard, H. B. (1955) A study of normative and informational social influences upon individual judgement. *Journal of Abnormal and Social Psychology*, 51, 629–36.

9 Perrin and Spencer kicked off the controversy with the following short article: Perrin, S. and Spencer, C. (1980) The Asch effect – a child of its time? *Bulletin of the British Psychological Society*, 32, 405–6.

10 Asch's letter which contains this quote is in the *British Journal of Social Psychology*, 1981, 20, 223.

11 See in the correspondence pages of the *Bulletin of the British Psychological Society*, January to April 1981.

12 These studies are fully reported in: Perrin, S. and Spencer, C. (1981) Independence and conformity in the Asch experiment. *British Journal of Social Psychology*, 20, 205–9.

13 This study is described in: Nicholson, N., Cole, S. G. and Rocklin, T. (1985) Conformity in the Asch situation: A comparison between contemporary British and US university students. *British Journal of Social Psychology*, 24, 59–63.

14 See note 4.

15 See note 5.

16 A very good overview of this research is Chapter 8 of: Raven, B. H. and Rubin, J. Z. (1983) *Social Psychology*. 2nd edn. New York: John Wiley.

17 For a good recent review of research in conformity pressures, see Chapter 6 of: Hogg, M. A. and Vaughan, G. M. (1995) *Social Psychology: An introduction*. Hemel Hempstead: Prentice Hall.

18 This quote and this line of argument is from Moscovici and describes

how his research and ideas developed over the years, in the foreword to a recent special edition of the *British Journal of Social Psychology* (1996) 35, Part 1 devoted to research on minority influence. For a more detailed description of the theory, see his 1980 or 1985 publications: Moscovici, S. (1980) Towards a theory of conversion behaviour. In Berkowitz, L. (ed.) *Advances in Experimental Social Psychology*. London: Academic Press; Moscovici, S. (1985) Social influence and conformity. In Lindzey, G. and Aronson, E. (eds) *The Handbook of Social Psychology*. 3rd edn. New York: Random House; Moscovici, S. (1996) Foreword. Just remembering. *British Journal of Social Psychology*, 35, 5–14.

19 This is a healthy reminder that all social research takes place in a given social context and may ignore views which do not seem to fit in with the prevailing social climate. For this quote and further background on this development, see: Nemeth, C. (1996) Editorial. *British Journal of Social Psychology*, 35, 1–3.

20 For a more detailed presentation of Nemeth's ideas, see: Nemeth, C. J. (1986) Differential contributions of majority and minority influence. *Psychological Review*, 93, 23–32; Nemeth, C. J. (1992) Minority influence as a stimulant to group [performance]. In Worchel, S., Wood, W. and Simpson, J. A. (1992) *Group Process and Productivity*. Newbury Park, CA: Sage. 95–111.

21 For an interesting example which also gives a very clear explanation of the differences between the two explanations, see: Martin, R. (1996) Minority influence and argument generation. *British Journal of Social Psychology*, 35, 91–103.

22 This study is: Van Dynne, L. and Saavedra, R. (1996) Minority influence in work-groups. *British Journal of Social Psychology*, 35, 151–67.

23 Quote from page 164 of the article by Van Dynne and Saavedra (note 22).

Chapter 6

Who wants to be leader?

This chapter investigates the 'problem' of leadership. Despite the enormous literature on the topic of leadership, both from practitioners and social scientists, we still do *not* have a definitive account of what it means to be an 'effective' leader across a wide range of situations. Of course, this may be because the concept is too complicated to allow a single or simple answer and this chapter will explore many of these complications.

To shed light on both the practical and theoretical mysteries of leadership, this chapter summarises major theories that have been used to explain it. As well as referring to popular images of leadership, this chapter will also assess recent trends in leadership research and relate these trends to other sections of this book.

What makes a leader – a tale of many literatures

There is no one body of literature sitting neatly in one place on your local library shelf which will uncover the mystery of leadership. This is partly because virtually every branch of social science considers it to be one of their topics – from political science through sociology and on to psychology. Add in the literature from management and business studies, stir with a liberal shake of practitioners telling us how they did it right, and you have a bewildering cocktail of often contradictory recipes.

To further illustrate the diversity of possible sources, read the following quote and try to guess its origins before you read on:

Leadership involves getting things done through people. How well you do this, this will be determined by your ability to communicate. . . . . other than your own personal communication methods there is one primary way that a section can communicate with its members. The primary way is through: Meetings!

This interesting advice is taken from the 'Communication and Meetings' subsection of the confidential charter of a leading Chicago street gang.[1]

What do you believe about leadership?

Before we wade into the mountain of research and theory on leadership that has emerged over the last few decades, it is worth thinking about *your* assumptions and expectations of what leadership involves. Try working through the following three questions – scribble a few notes to summarise your responses – and then see how your opinions and feelings relate to the theories we cover in the rest of this chapter.

Who would you regard as an effective leader?

When I ask student groups this question, the discussion invariably starts by considering major public figures. How do you feel about your present Prime Minister or President? Does he/she match up to the previous occupants of the post? And what about major figures in world history? What is your verdict on Napoleon, John Kennedy, Martin Luther King, Winston Churchill etc.? Should we be modelling our present leadership behaviour on the example set by Attila the Hun who summarised his new leadership style in AD 450 as follows:

> Among you Chieftains and Huns will be those whose spirits cling to our past ways. We will show patience with you unenlightened ones. Yet, if you choose not our new course and cause dissension, you will be stricken from our ranks.

You can use your own imagination to consider what 'being stricken' might involve at the hands of Attila. You might decide to dismiss this last approach as such techniques might be a little drastic by today's standards. Before you do, I would remind you that one of the best-selling recent management texts on leadership was a modern revision of the words and philosophy of Attila.[2]

Casting historical legends aside for a moment, what about the people you meet in your everyday life – which of these do you consider a leader, and why?

Do you want to be a leader?

When I deliver a lecture on leadership, I always start by asking the audience this question and asking for a show of hands. Here in England, I get a fairly predictable response from undergraduate students – there is a ripple of embarrassment, then everyone looks around at one another, then a few hands move confidently into the air and then a few more rather gingerly move upwards. Out of 100 students, I do not expect to see more than 10 hands in the air! Is this a function of the situation where people feel embarrassed in such a large gathering or is this a genuine self-assessment? Would I get the same reaction in other cultures as in America or Japan? What was your reaction to this question?

What are the essential characteristics of leadership?

Take a few minutes to decide how far you agree or disagree with the following quotes from a recent book by Michael Shea.[3] Shea's career has covered academia, business, politics and diplomacy, including a nine-year spell as press secretary to the Queen. So, from his experience of meeting some of the most powerful people in this country if not the world, can he provide the answers to the critical issues surrounding the leadership process?

For example, he is convinced that that leaders are critical to an organisation or group's success:

> One man or woman with exceptional abilities, when faced with exactly the same team previously run by a poor manager, can transform a company, a political party or even a country. A team can climb an impossible mountain if properly led.

This view has considerable popular support, at the very least among the directors and owners of sports clubs. In British football, the manager's is always the head to roll when results are not going well, and this is a pattern repeated across the world. To reinforce this policy, every year we can find examples of teams which do seem to have rediscovered how to hit the ball after the appointment of a new manager.

Shea is equally clear that leaders have distinctive skills, qualities and functions:

> Of the 'three C's' of leadership, Communication, Confidence and Charisma, the first two can be developed . . . the elusive quality of charisma cannot be 'learned', however.

What do researchers believe about leadership?

I selected the above quotes from Shea's book for three main reasons. First, it is written by someone who has very wide experience of different organisations and different examples of leadership behaviour. Second, there are a number of texts which offer to 'reveal . . . the rules and tricks of the leadership game'.[4] Shea's is a fairly typical example. It offers a coherent and well-argued view of leadership which does seem to have a fair degree of popular acceptance. The key points include:

- leaders have special qualities
- we can train leaders to some extent
- leaders have an important effect on their organisations
- we need leaders, and only one leader in each situation

Third, these views of leadership are not shared by some of the researchers who have worked on these issues over the last few decades. Many researchers do not believe that we really understand enough about leadership to offer the confident advice that comes from Michael Shea. For example, consider the following contrasting quotes:

> The essence of leadership remains as elusive as ever.[5]

> the models of leadership that have found most favour have been ones which embody the implicit value-systems of Western advanced industrial cultures.[6]

Other authors have been even more negative and dismissive of the voluminous research literature on leadership, arguing that we have precious little to show for so much work.[7]

Before we return to these issues, we shall journey through the main approaches which researchers have adopted in the quest for the secrets of leadership.

The search for the personality traits and characteristics which underpin leadership

In terms of systematic research studies, this is the longest established line of research into the leadership process. It is also an idea with a very long history: some textbooks start their discussion of leadership traits with quotations from Aristotle. There have been a number of comprehensive reviews of the studies carried out over the last seventy years. For example, based on a review of 163 trait studies, Stogdill concluded that the following profile is characteristic of successful leaders:

> The leader is characterized by a strong drive for responsibility and task completion, rigor, and persistence in pursuit of goals, venturesomeness and originality in problem solving, drive to exercise initiative in social situations, self-confidence and sense of personal identity, willingness to accept consequences of decision and action, readiness to absorb interpersonal stress, willingness to tolerate frustration and delay, ability to influence other persons' behaviour, and capability to structure social interaction systems to the purpose at hand.[8]

However, most of the summaries of the work done in this area conclude that this approach does not provide much of an answer. Typical problems reported are:

Weak relationship

The relationship between effective leadership and personality traits has not been very strong. The studies have usually tried to correlate leadership ratings with personality ratings. For example, one early review by Mann[9] found no correlation higher than 0.25. A score of 1.0 would mean a perfect relationship where there is an exact match between ratings of effective leadership and specific personality traits. No relation would give a correlation of 0.

Different traits

There is a lack of consistency between studies. Different studies have reported that different traits are important.

Dramatic exceptions

Whatever the list of traits which has emerged it is possible to find a dramatic example of someone who was an effective leader yet did not possess these traits.

These difficulties led many researchers to the conclusion that different settings must require a different type of person to be an effective leader and attention swung to the sorts of activities or functions we could expect leaders to perform in given situations.

The resurgence of personality

However, we cannot simply consign this view to the category of historical blind alley. It is still very persistent in the 'how to do it' literature on leadership, although these texts often suggest that leaders must have a specific mix, not just of personality traits, but of personality, skills and abilities. For example, Shea[10] concludes that leaders must have the following ten qualities: a 'clear, strong sense of mission'; flexible obstinacy; opportunism; self-assurance; substance (there must be something substantial to the leader rather than just a good 'image'); endurance; inspiration (the ability to inspire others); communication skills; good judgement; and ambition 'that extra push, that extra burst of energy to take them over the top'.

One difficulty with this approach is this tendency to mix up personality traits, skills and abilities. This mix of qualities is also found in the research reviews: for example, see the quote from Stogdill given earlier. This also suggests that the approach is far from forgotten when you consider that one of the main devices used in industry and commerce to select future leaders is the assessment centre, where managers are put through simulated exercises and their performance is evaluated in relation to personality measures.

There is also the possibility which is implied in Shea's notion of 'substance' that followers will not accept someone as their leader unless they conform to a particular personality profile. So we can expect that there would be some consistency in leader personalities in given situations as a function of follower acceptance, and this is one area that has received renewed attention. There is also a more radical extension of this view which suggests that people have a romanticised view of leadership which means they exaggerate its impact and importance. From this point of view, leadership 'emerges as a state of mind within the follower'.[11]

New studies of personality

Moving back to more conventional ideas, there have been a number of studies over the last fifteen years which suggest that there might be more stability in the traits associated with effective leadership than previously supposed. For example, reanalysis of some of the earlier work like Mann's has come up with higher correlations.[12]

This does not imply that researchers want to resurrect the idea that personality is *the* key variable. Rather it means that several researchers have developed more elaborate theories of leadership which give more importance to the personality of the leader, and how this is perceived by followers. For example, Lord and colleagues have developed an information-processing approach which examines how leaders and followers categorise the personality traits they expect in the leader.[13] They found that people expected leaders to have some traits like intelligence across virtually all situations. Other expectations were much more specific.

Charisma rides again

Finally, in this section, it is worth mentioning the recent revival of interest in studies of so-called charismatic leadership. This is the idea that some leaders can inspire extraordinary levels of trust and devotion from their followers simply by having a very special 'charismatic' personality. The idea has a long history in politics and sociology but has only recently been studied in more detail from a behavioural point of view.

There certainly are some situations where followers do react very emotionally to their leaders and where that leader is seen as having very special qualities. What is not so clear is how and why these attachments and perceptions develop. Perhaps the most immediate practical implication of this research is looking at some of the techniques which are used by charismatic leaders to inspire their followers.[14]

The search for leadership functions

Looking at what leaders did took a number of directions, one of which was to try to define the functions of leadership. This approach can be illustrated with two important initiaitives, one from the USA and one from the UK.

The Ohio State studies

One of the most important American research programmes in this area became known as the Ohio State leadership studies.[15] These studies suggested that leaders carried out two main functions which they termed initiating structure and consideration. Initiating structure includes defining the group's goals and objectives and organising the members' tasks and activities. Consideration involves concern for the welfare of subordinates and work to create good personal relationships across the group.

At first sight, these two functions look similar if not identical to the task/socio-emotional distinction we introduced in Chapter 3 in the discussion of Bales's work. There is one important difference – Bales saw these two functions as inversely related. In other words, if you score high on one you score low on the other. The Ohio studies proposed that effective leaders would could score highly on both dimensions. Although subsequent research in this tradition came up with less conclusive results, this notion became the basis of recommendations for effective leadership which we return to later in this chapter.

Action-centred leadership

In the UK, the work of John Adair has been adopted as a model for leadership training in a wide variety of organisations, not just industrial and commercial ones.[16] He has argued strongly that British education and society must take the issue of good leadership much more seriously. In 1991, in an article advocating the establishment of an Institute of Leadership Studies, he concluded that:

> As a nation we do need to think deeply and clearly about the nature of leadership at its different levels and 'education for leadership' . . . We must give more attention to how to develop good leaders – and leaders for good.[17]

Adair's model proposes that leaders fulfil three functions:[18]

- achieving the task
- building the team, maintaining good working relationships throughout the team
- developing the individuals in the team, dealing with the members' needs as individuals

The first two of these are akin to the task/socio-emotional division we have already met. It is perhaps ironic that the third area is often neglected in American models of effective leadership despite the strong individualistic emphasis in American culture. Adair regards all these areas as critical and interrelated.

And the practitioner's view

Again you will find an array of functions advocated by practitioners. For example, Shea[19] talks of leaders carrying out the following functions: initiating; articulating; inspiring; monitoring; and role setting.

The search for leadership style

If we know what leaders do then perhaps we can also define an ideal leader style. Two main studies can illustrate this approach:

Is democratic leadership the best?

The classic study which aimed to define the effects of different styles of leadership, including the democratic style, was done by Lewin, Lippitt and White.[20] They trained youth leaders in three styles of leadership and then rotated them among groups making aeroplane models in a boys' club to see which style had the greatest impact. The three styles were:

- authoritarian, where the leader decided what the group should do, assigned tasks, did not consult before making decisions, and did not participate in the group activities
- democratic, where the leader consulted the group before making decisions and participated in the group activities
- laissez-faire, where the leader adopted a 'laid-back' style and let the group do more or less what it wanted

Many textbooks have reported this study in a way which suggests that democratic leadership was unequivocally the 'best'. This is not a very full picture of the results. The democratic groups did report the highest morale and satisfaction, kept working even when the leader was absent, and produced the highest quality models. The autocratic groups produced the most models but only when the leader was present. When the autocratic leaders were absent, their groups quickly turned to misbehaviour as their preferred activity.

Later studies produced mixed results, some favouring democratic and some favouring autocratic leadership.[21]

The Managerial Grid

Blake and Mouton took the ideas of task and socio-emotional leadership behaviours and developed them into an influential programme of training and organisational development.[22] They proposed that the most effective managers were those who scored highly on both these dimensions which they called concern for production and concern for people. Using a 9-point scale for each, they developed a matrix illustrating the various styles, known as the Managerial Grid. The ideal style is the '9+9' style where the leader scores the maximum on both concerns.

One of their most interesting contributions is a fundamental critique of the Ohio model which treats the two dimensions as independent of one another. They argue that the two dimensions are always interrelated. For example, a subordinate will respond to a manager's task behaviours in terms of that manager's past and present actions on the socio-emotional side. If someone treats you with consideration and respect, then you are more likely to respond positively to them when they ask you to 'do this job this way'.

Contingency approaches

Given that research on style and functions did not always deliver consistent results, researchers turned to more complex models, suggesting that effective leadership is contingent on a number of factors. This view can be illustrated by the work of Fred Fiedler who developed probably the most famous and still the most controversial of these models.

Fiedler's contingency theory

One of the most widely quoted contingency theories of leadership was first developed by Fred Fiedler in the 1960s.[23] He accepted the idea from Bales that there were two types of leader – task and socio-emotional – and that these two types were taken on by different types of people. He developed a questionnaire called the Least

Preferred Co-worker scale (LPC) which he claims is a reliable measure of these two different leadership types. If you try the LPC you are asked to think of the one person with whom you have found it most difficult to work. You are then asked to rate this person on a number of bipolar scales (friendly/unfriendly, pleasant/unpleasant etc.). The assumption is that, if you are a socio-emotional leader, then you will tend to see even difficult people in positive terms and you will achieve a high LPC score when all your ratings are added up. The opposite is true for task leaders. Because you are so committed to the task then you will tend to see difficult people in negative terms and you will achieve a low LPC score when all your ratings are added up. This LPC scale has been controversial and we shall outline some of the criticisms later.

With a measure of the leader's style, Fiedler then went on to see which style was effective in which situation. He suggested that there were three key dimensions of what he called situational control, the amount of control which the situation allows the leader to exert over the group. These three dimensions were the affective relations between the leader and the members – how they liked each other – the degree of structure to the task facing the group, and the position power of the leader. The position power is the amount of authority which the leader can use legitimately in the situation. For example, does the leader have the power to make a member leave the group?

Given that each one of these dimensions could be low or high (good or poor), then this gives eight different permutations ranging from highly favourable in situation 1 – where the leader has most control – to highly unfavourable – where the leader has least control – in situation 8. These eight permutations are listed in Table 17.[24]

Table 17

Situation	Position power	Task structure	Leader/ member relations
1	High	High	Good
2	Low	High	Good
3	High	Low	Good
4	Low	Low	Good
5	High	High	Poor
6	Low	High	Poor
7	High	Low	Poor
8	Low	Low	Poor

Fiedler than went on to conduct and survey research on effective leadership using this model and concluded that:

- Task leadership is most effective where situational control is extremely high or extremely low (as in situations 1, 2 and 8).
- Socio-emotional leadership is most effective where situational control is intermediate (as in situations 4, 5 and 6).

Situations 3 and 7 are less clear-cut although Fiedler usually advocates task-oriented leadership for 3, socio-emotional leadership for 7. He has produced an impressive array of evidence to support these conclusions but there are a number of important issues to raise which might limit its application to every group everywhere. One important development is his training programme described below which adopts a very different stance to most leadership development programmes.

Evaluating Fiedler

There are at least four critical questions which we must throw at Fiedler's theory.[25] At the moment, there are reservations on all these issues which suggest that Fiedler's approach does not yet offer the definitive account of leadership which he claims:

- What does the LPC scale really measure? It is based on a relationship between our perceptions of others and our own behaviour which has been questioned.
- How fixed is leader style? Fiedler treats it as fixed but this contradicts other evidence that humans can be very flexible.
- Are all possible situations covered by his three dimensions? Are there not other characteristics which are important in some situations, like the relationship of your group to other groups?
- What about the process/development of leadership? The notion that leadership is a developing process seems to be ignored by Fiedler's theory.

Other contingency models

There are a range of contingency models apart from Fiedler's which emphasise different aspects of the situation.[26] A couple of examples will illustrate some of the differences:

Hersey and Blanchard's Situational Leadership

The main factor which they incorporate into their model which has not been mentioned before is what they term the maturity of the group members.[27] Where this is high, the members are prepared to take on jobs and use their initiative; where this is low, members will wait to be instructed and will not have the confidence to carry on themselves.

They provide a model which links the leader's style and behaviour to the group members' level of maturity. The leadership will be effective if the leader's style of interaction is appropriate to the members. For example, with high maturity members, leaders can delegate; with low maturity members, leaders must be able to instruct or tell. Where the maturity is intermediate then leaders must be able to use participative or more directive methods depending on their needs.

Although this theory does not seem to have generated much supporting research it seems very popular with trainers and personnel specialists. Unfortunately, the message from this chapter and other research summaries is that any simple model of leadership behaviour is almost certainly mistaken.[28]

Misumi's PM leadership theory

One important aspect of this theory is that it was developed in Japan and demonstrates a concern with cultural variables which is often ignored in Western approaches.[29]

Misumi starts from familiar ground by distinguishing between two leadership functions which he describes as performance and maintenance. Performance includes the task functions like deciding the goals; maintenance includes the social functions like supporting the members and maintaining good relations. This gives rise to four main styles of leadership:

- PM includes both performance and maintenance behaviours
- P emphasises performance behaviours
- M emphasises maintenance behaviours
- pm emphasises neither

So is this not an oriental version of Blake and Mouton? It is in fact very different. Misumi's research showed that PM leaders are not like the '9+9' leaders of the Managerial Grid: they are much more moderate on each dimension, more like a '5+5' pattern which Blake and Mouton see as less effective. According to Misumi, the most effective leaders in terms of both productive and satisfied groups are the PM type, followed by M, then P and finally the pm style.

Another important difference in this theory is the emphasis on the different meaning attached to similar behaviours in different settings. For example, suppose I am your boss and I suggest a different way of doing one of your jobs. If you are a new employee, you will probably accept this as helpful and supportive; if you are a long-serving employee, you may find me intrusive or pressurising or helpful depending on our existing relationship. So the underlying dimensions of P and M are still the same but their expression needs to vary.

Finally it is worth re-emphasising Misumi's concern for cultural differences. He claims that his conclusions are only valid for Japanese managers and further research has modified his model in other cultures. Peterson reports a Chinese development – CPM – which uses PM but adds a third dimension – C – for moral character.[30] However, Western researchers have increasingly become interested in both the applications and implications of Misumi's work.[31]

Leadership and 'image'

There is ample evidence that many of the important figures of our day have spent a lot of time (and presumably even more money) to improve their public performances in, for example, TV interviews: the debate about the influence of television on the American presidential elections has been buzzing ever since the classic confrontation between Kennedy and Nixon in the 1960s. For an example of how politicians can modify their appearance and style to improve their image, compare the early and later media interviews given by the then British Prime Minister Margaret Thatcher.

The training dilemma

Given that we have different and possibly conflicting models of leadership, it is not surprising that we have different models of leadership training. There are two broad approaches:

The 'best way'

There are training programmes which aim to instruct you in some 'best way' of acting as a leader, either by showing you an ideal style or by demonstrating flexible approaches to cope with different followers. Examples include the Managerial Grid from the USA and Action-Centred Leadership in the UK.

Doctoring the situation

The opposing viewpoint is that you should adjust the situation, as your style is difficult to modify. The most influential example of this comes from Fiedler and is worth explaining in more detail.

The Fiedler training programme

Fiedler describes basic leadership style as 'part of your personality'. To change it is as difficult 'as suddenly trying to become a completely different person'.[32] Thus, he recommends that you should change your situation if you want to achieve a better match between your style and the characteristics of your situation.

His manual provides both detailed questionnaires which enable you to assess the characteristics of your situation and suggestions for revising the situation. For example, you can change the leader–member relations by either increasing or decreasing the morale and rapport with the team. Similarly, you can change task structure through more or less detailed planning. Positive power can also be manipulated, either by using or relaxing whatever rules or sanctions are available in the situation.

One criticism here is that manipulating these situations or characteristics may require you to take on different behaviours – surely also related to your personality which Fiedler regards as so difficult to change.

Leadership and management

Another important issue is the difference between leadership and management, often discriminated in the way summarised in Table 18. The general distinction is between the notions of 'direction' and 'vision' associated with leadership and notions of 'competence' and 'efficient operations' associated with management.[33] This is often

Table 18

The leader	The manager
Creates and communicates the vision	Controls
Develops power base	Is appointed
Initiates and leads change	Maintains status quo
Sets objectives	Concentrates on results

summarised in the catchphrase 'leaders are people who do the right things and managers are people who do things right.'[34]

Certainly authors like Adair use this distinction to characterise leaders. For example, he concludes that Nelson was a great manager rather than leader whereas Margaret Thatcher was just the opposite.[35]

Another way of dealing with this distinction is to say that leadership is simply one of the many roles which managers may play. One influential example of this approach is the work of Henry Mintzberg. He suggests that managers can occupy ten roles: three interpersonal roles, including leader; three informational roles, including monitor and disseminator of information, and four decisional roles, including negotiator and entrepreneur.[36] This concern with the roles associated with leadership is just one of the important recent trends in leadership research which we now turn to.

Recent developments in leadership research

The search for the definitive account of leadership shows no sign of abating and there a number of emerging and linked themes and issues. These are discussed below with some comments on their most important practical implications:

Vision, communication and networking

The flavour of new approaches which emphasise the leader's need to communicate a clear vision for the group or organisation is captured in the following quote from Howard Gardner:

A leader is an individual who creates a story – a mental representation – that significantly affects the thoughts, behaviours and feelings – the mental representations – of a significant number of persons (termed followers).[37]

From a study of the characteristics of twenty one 'leading leaders' such as Mahatma Gandhi, Margaret Thatcher, and Pope John XXIII, Gardner goes on to emphasise the communicative and educative functions of leadership. This emphasis on communication is also reflected in other recent characterisations of the effective leader. For example, a recent American survey which aimed to describe the skills required of the successful chief executive in the year 2000 concluded that the ability to convey a strong sense of vision was the most critical.[38] In the same vein, many recent management texts emphasise this need to communicate the organisational vision.[39] Corresponding to this concern with communication is the need for the effective leaders to build appropriate networks both within and outside the group.

Culture and values

Another related concern, especially in the literature on organisational leadership, is to emphasise the leader's role in building and maintaining an appropriate culture for the group to work in and for the leader to be concerned with values and goals. For example, Bennis and Nanus talk of leaders as 'designers of cultures';[40] in one of the most influential management texts of the last twenty years, Peters and Waterman coined the term 'cultures of excellence'.[41] The leader's role is critical in establishing such a culture.

Personalities, roles and competences

As well as the revived interest in personality characteristics mentioned earlier in this chapter, recent texts have advocated a more flexible and complex view of the roles and competences which leaders need to demonstrate.

For example, Robert Quinn and colleagues have developed what they call the competing values framework to summarise the four major perspectives on management:

- rational goal, emphasising achievement and effectiveness
- internal process, emphasising rules, control and coordination
- human relations, emphasising team commitment, cohesion and morale
- open systems, emphasising adaptability, external suppport, and internal/external networks

From these four values, they derive eight basic roles which 'help us to organise our thoughts about what is expected of a person holding a position of leadership'.[42] Of these eight roles required of manager leaders, two are associated with each value: director and producer (both associated with the rational goal perspective); coordinator and monitor (internal process); mentor and facilitator (human relations); innovator and broker (open systems).

Each role is based on specific competences. For example, the director role requires three: visioning, planning and goal setting; designing and organising; and delegating effectively.

Leadership as 'situated action'

This involves a more sophisticated analysis of the situations that leaders find themselves in than you find in earlier contingency theories. For example, Smith and Peterson suggest that leaders have to cope with a continuous flow of events which they have to respond to.[43] How effectively they respond will depend on the way that both leaders and followers interpret the situations and events. So the environment for the leader is not fixed or static as implied by other theories. Leadership training then becomes a matter of increasing the leaders' awareness of how they attend to information in the environment and how they decide which behaviours will achieve their objectives.

Another development which relates to this sort of approach is the increased concern with the characteristics of the followers. Rather than seeing followers as a homogenous mass, we must recognise that leader–member relations will be influenced by many variables, notably gender and ethnic background. We must also pay more attention to roles within the group, as discussed in Chapter 7.

Leadership as skilled behaviour

Researchers have become more interested in the detailed analysis of behaviours by leaders. For example, Wright and Taylor provide a very detailed analysis of the interpersonal skills required of leaders, describing them at three levels:[44]

- the primary components, such as the questions, statements and nonverbal behaviours which leaders use in interacting with followers

- the structural factors, which are the ways in which these primary components are used in sequence. For example, in an interview, you might want to start with an open general question followed by probes and closed questions (a funnel sequence) as opposed to starting with a very specific question and working out to more general issues (inverted funnel)
- the overall approach, which includes the level of friendliness and how far the leader is willing to let the follower influence the content of the interaction

According to this analysis, skilled leaders use an extensive range of the primary components, can structure and organise interactions effectively, and adopt an approach which enables them to achieve desired objectives and which is appropriate for the needs and perceptions of the followers involved.

Wright suggests that recent studies along these lines offer a fairly consistent view of effective leadership behaviour in that they:

> demonstrate the importance of gathering information, listening to other people's responses and avoiding such behaviours as negative evaluation, disagreeing, criticising and ignoring other people's contributions.[45]

If you want to check your behaviour as a leader (or your leader's behaviour), see how far these behaviour descriptions apply to your next meetings.

Cultural differences

Earlier in this chapter, I included a quote which suggested that much of the research done on leadership had neglected cultural differences and operated very much from Western perspectives.

For example, I summarised the boys' clubs study on leadership styles earlier in this chapter. A modified version of this was done in Japan and found quite different results. The different consequences of democratic and autocratic leadership seemed to depend on the difficulty of the task. With easy tasks, the democratic style was more effective; with difficult tasks, the autocratic style was more effective. A similar study in India found the autocratic style more effective on all tasks.[46]

One suggestion that has emerged fom cross-cultural research like Misumi's is that there may be some common qualities required of leaders in many cultures but that the way these are expressed will be very different. For example, how leaders express concern and respect for their followers will depend on cultural and situational norms which can be very different.

Subcultural differences and bias: the example of gender

The problem with many of the recipes for effective leadership is that they ignore the cultural difficulties experienced by women who take on a professional leadership role. Jamieson tells of the double bind dilemmas which women face.[47] A double bind is where whatever choice you make, you lose. Shirley Williams gives the following example:

> If a woman is a full-time wife and mother, her neighbour at dinner will assume she has nothing interesting to say. If she has a full-time occupation, either she has ruthlessly cut off the life of feeling and emotion or else she neglects her children and exploits her husband.[48]

Gender issues may well be especially important in specific situations. For example, the notion that different leadership styles are appropriate for different situations is still very much alive. Rodrigues has argued that you can identify three types of leadership: innovators, implementors, and pacifiers.[49] These are linked to the three problem phases which organisations experience. When an organisation needs an injection of new ideas then an innovator is needed; when an organisation needs to implement proposals, it needs an implementor and when the organisation has reached a stable state, it needs a pacifier.

Rodrigues noted that managers he worked with felt that these styles were gender based and that 'our society allows males, but not females, to play the innovator role, that females are tied mainly to the pacifier role'.

It is no coincidence that recent texts in leadership and management have paid more attention to this issue. For example, Shackleton reports that women often make better leaders than men as they can more comfortably integrate concern for the task with concern for the group members.[50] However, they may also confront more barriers to taking on leadership roles and be placed under different and more onerous pressures than men when they do achieve a given leadership position.

Coming back to groups

One way of making use (and sense) of this research is to see how we can apply the main ideas to a specific group situation. Suppose you have just gone along to the first meeting of a new local group which has been formed to raise funds for a worthy local venture. The person who has called the meeting has very definitely announced that they are not interested in taking on the leadership role. You are committed to the project. Could you be leader?

Using some of the research from this chapter, we can generate some self-test questions to assess your chances and the actions you would need to focus on if the leadership role became yours:

- How are you perceived by the other members of the group?
- What leadership style would the group members expect and/or accept? Are they looking for very clear task direction or more of a coordinating role?
- Can you effectively communicate the desired goals and objectives both within and outside the group? Do you have a clear vision which members will find convincing?
- What would your position be in the group? For example, consider Fiedler's situation characteristics. Could you require a member to leave?

Some of these questions cannot be answered simply by reflecting upon leadership research. Compare your answers to these questions now with the way you would respond after also considering the content of the next chapter where we review issues of structure and communication.

Notes

1 Quotes on page 33 of Dwight Conquerhood's analysis of gang communication: Conquerhood, D. (1994) Homeboys and hoods: Gang communication and cultural space. In Frey, L. R. (ed.) *Group Communication in Context*. Hillsdale, NJ: Lawrence Erlbaum Associates.
2 Wess Roberts turned Attila the Hun into a contemporary management guru in 1989: Roberts, W. (1989) *The Leadership Secrets of Attila the Hun*. New York: Bantam.
3 For the quotes on this and the next page, see pages 113ff. of Shea, M. (1990) *Leadership Rules*. London: Century.
4 This quote is taken from the dust jacket of Shea's book.
5 Quote from page 1 of: Leavy, B. and Wilson, D. (1994) *Strategy and Leadership*. London: Routledge.

6 Quote from page 1 of: Smith, P. B. and Peterson, M. F. (1988) *Leadership, Organizations and Culture*. London: Sage.

7 For a collection of articles offering a pessimistic view of leadership research, see: McCall, M. W. and Lombardo, M. M. (eds) (1978) *Leadership: Where else can we go?* Durham, NC: Duke University Press.

8 The most comprehensive survey of leadership studies up until the early 1970s was Stogdill's Handbook, which belied its modest title with well over 1,000 pages. This quote is taken from page 81 of the Handbook. This has now been revised by Bass. The conclusion that personality traits do not account for much of the variability in leaders' behaviour can be found in the reviews by Yukl (1981) and Bryman (1986): Bass, B. M. (1990) *Bass and Stogdill's Handbook of Leadership: Theory, research and managerial applications*, 3rd edn. New York: Free Press; Bryman, A. (1986) *Leadership and Organisations*. London: Routledge & Kegan Paul; Stogdill, R. M. (1974) *Handbook of Leadership*. New York: Free Press; Yukl, G. A. (1981) *Leadership in Organisations*. Englewood Cliffs, NJ: Prentice Hall.

9 For a reassessment of Mann's 1959 study and related research, see Wright page 170ff. (note 12).

10 See Chapter 3 of the book by Shea (note 3).

11 This quote is taken from a discussion of the work of Meindl on page 59 of the excellent book by Shackleton. If you want to examine contemporary ideas on leadership in more detail then my 'top three' recommendations would be Shackleton, Wright (note 12) and Smith and Peterson (note 6): Shackleton, V. (1995) *Business Leadership*. London: Routledge.

12 See Chapter 8 of an excellent overview of leadership research by Peter Wright: Wright, P. (1995) *Managerial Leadership*. London: Routledge.

13 See: Lord, R. G. and Maher, K. J. (1993) *Leadership and Information Processing: Linking perceptions and performance*. London: Routledge.

14 See Chapter 9 of Wright's book (note 12).

15 A comprehensive review of studies on the Ohio State approach is: Kerr, S. and Schriesheim, C. (1974) Consideration, initiating structure and organisational criteria – An update of Korman's review. *Personnel Psychology*, 27, 555–68.

16 For a discussion of leadership in higher education which incorporates Adair's model and other issues which provide interesting perspectives on issues in this chapter, see: Brodie, D. and Partington, P. (1992) *HE Departmental Leadership/Management: An exploration of roles and responsibilities*. Sheffield: USDU/CVCP.

17 See the article: Adair, J. (1991) Quest for lost leaders. *Times Higher Education Supplement*, 26 July, p. 16.

18 You can find Adair's approach in various texts: Adair, J. (1979) *Action-Centred Leadership*. London: Gower; Adair, J. (1983) *Effective Leadership*. London: Gower and Pan; Adair, J. (1984) *Skills of Leadership*. London: Gower.

19 See Chapter 4 of the book by Shea (note 3).

20 Lewin's study rightly became recognised as a classic study within

social psychology. It is still worth reading even though it is now over half a century old. For a more recent discussion of its implications, see the book by Lippitt and White: Lewin, K., Lippitt, R. and White, R. K. (1939) Patterns of aggressive behaviour in experimentally created social climates. *Journal of Social Psychology*, 10, 271–99; White, R. K. and Lippitt, R. (1960) *Autocracy and Democracy*. New York: Harper.

21 For examples of more recent research on the impact of leadership style, see the discussion in pages 8ff. of Smith and Peterson (note 6).

22 The detail of Blake and Mouton's approach can be found in their main text, first issued in 1964 and revised in 1978. For a brief critical review, see page 44ff. of Wright (note 12). More recently Blake has added a third dimension to cover motivational aspects of the styles: Blake, R. R. and Mouton, J. S. (1964) *The Managerial Grid*. Houston, TX: Gulf; Blake, R. R. and Mouton, J. S. (1978) *The New Managerial Grid*. Houston, TX: Gulf; Blake, R. R. and McCanse, A. A. (1991) *Leadership Dilemmas – Grid Solutions*. Houston, TX: Gulf.

23 Fiedler's now classic text is: Fiedler, F. E. (1967) *A Contingency Theory of Leadership Effectiveness*. New York: McGraw-Hill.

24 For a fuller description of Fiedler's model which also includes an example of an LPC scale, see pages 430ff. of: Feldman, R. S. (1995) *Social Psychology*. Englewood Cliffs, NJ: Prentice-Hall.

25 For main criticisms of Fiedler, see pages 49ff. of Wright (note 12).

26 For a review of other contingency models, see Chapter 4 of Wright (note 12).

27 Hersey and Blanchard's model is reviewed in many general texts in social psychology or you can use their own text: Hersey, P. and Blanchard, K. H. (1982) *Management of Organizational Behaviour: Utilising human resources*. 4th edn Englewood Cliffs, NJ: Prentice Hall.

28 For a brief critical review of Hersey and Blanchard's model, see pages 59ff. of Wright (note 12).

29 For the full description of PM theory, see Misumi's 1985 book. For a summary and discussion of implications, see the article by Misumi and Peterson: Misumi, J. (1985) *The Behavioural Science of Leadership: An interdisciplinary Japanese research program*. Ann Arbor, MI: University of Michigan Press; Misumi, J. and Peterson, M. F. (1985) The Performance-Maintenance (PM) theory of leadership: Review of a Japanese research program. *Administrative Science Quarterly*, 30, 198–223.

30 This is discussed in: Peterson, M. F. (1988) PM Theory in Japan and China: What's in it for the United States? *Organizational Dynamics*, 16, 22–38.

31 For example see the discussion in Wright, pages 72–9 (note 12) and the book by Smith and Peterson (note 6).

32 See page 152 of Fiedler's training manual, first published in 1976: Fiedler, F. E. and Chemers, M. M. (1984) *Improving Leadership Effectiveness: The Leader Match Concept*, revised edition. New York: Wiley.

33 See in Middlehurst (note 35 below).

34 From page 6 of a book which emphasises the need for leaders to focus on vision, development and innovation: Bennis, W. and Townsend, R. (1996) *Reinventing Leadership*. London: Piatkus.

35 For a more detailed discussion of the distinction, see Adair. For a discussion of what it can mean in a specific organisational context, see Middlehurst: Adair, J. (1989) *Great Leaders*. London: Talbot Adair Press; Middlehurst, R. (1991) *The Changing Roles of University Leaders and Managers*. Sheffield: CVCP/USDU.

36 See the book by Mintzberg or the summary in Wright, Chapter 2 (note 12): Mintzberg, H. (1973) *The Nature of Managerial Work*. New York: Harper and Row.

37 This quote is taken from Howard Gardner's 1995 article, page 15, which offers a summary of the main themes of his book: Gardner, H. (1995) Self-raising power. *Times Higher Education Supplement*, 28 July, p. 15; Gardner, H. (1996) *Leading Minds*. London: HarperCollins.

38 This survey is reported in: Korn, L. B. (1989) How the next CEO will be different. *Fortune*, 22 May, p. 175.

39 See the books by Quigley or Bennis and Nanus: Quigley, J. V. (1993) *Vision. How leaders develop it, share it and sustain it*. New York: McGraw-Hill; Bennis, W. G. and Nanus, B. (1985) *Leaders: the strategies for taking charge*. New York: Harper and Row.

40 See note 34.

41 This book became a management best-seller and gave rise to several 'sequels': Peters, T. J. and Waterman, R. H. (1982) *In Search of Excellence*. New York: Harper and Row.

42 Quoted from page 23 of this book which contains materials to help readers work on their own competences. A self-assessment guide is also available: Quinn, R. E., Faerman, S. R., Thompson, M. P. and McGrath, M. R. (1996) *Becoming a Master Manager: A competency framework*. 2nd edn. New York: John Wiley.

43 Smith and Peterson present this event management model in their book (note 6).

44 Wright and Taylor introduced their approach in 1984 in the book which is now in its second edition. For a discussion of the implications of this approach, see their 1985 article: Wright, P. L. and Taylor, D. S. (1994) *Improving Leadership Performance: Interpersonal skills for effective leadership*. 2nd edn. Hemel Hempstead: Prentice-Hall; Wright, P. L. and Taylor, D. S. (1985) The implication of a skills approach to leadership. *Journal of Management Development*, 4, 15–28.

45 See page 123 of Wright (note 12).

46 See the article by Misumi and Peterson (note 29).

47 See: Jamieson, K. H. (1995) *Beyond the Double Bind*. Oxford: Oxford University Press.

48 This quote comes from Shirley Williams' review of Jamieson's book in the *Times Higher Educational Supplement*, 24 November 1995.

49 See: Rodrigues, C. A. (1993) Developing three-dimensional leaders. *Journal of Management Development*, 12, 3, 4–11.

50 See Chapter 11 of Shackleton (note 11).

Chapter 7

Who does what? Structure and communication

Every group which survives for any length of time develops a structure which has a number of different dimensions. In order to understand what is going on in the group, we need to understand these structural dimensions. We need to observe how they work, both independently and in relation to one another:

- power, status and authority
- liking
- roles

These are examined in turn before looking at some relevant work on communication in groups. Finally, this chapter returns to the issue of how we can integrate (or not) the different findings.

Power, status and authority

One of the most challenging exercises which is sometimes used in group training is to ask the members of the group to line themselves up in a way which represents their relative power or status in the group. Imagine doing this exercise with a group which you are a member of: what would be the result? How would members react?

This exercise *cannot* be recommended as a 'fun game' to while away some idle group time. The fact is that it will almost inevitably stir up very strong emotions and reactions in group members and this reinforces one main point of this chapter: groups do develop status hierarchies, and these hierarchies can be very important and sometimes very destructive.

Different power structures

One line of research has been to identify different types of power which we can exert over one another. The typical list distinguishes five types:[1]

- reward, whereby I have power over you because I can give you certain rewards.
- coercive, whereby I have power over you because I can punish you or threaten you in certain ways.
- legitimate, whereby I have power over you because you recognise that this is fair or legitimate. This is really the notion of authority which we discuss separately later on.
- referent, whereby I have power over you because you identify with me or wish to be like me in certain ways. Fan worship or adulation is a common example of referent power.
- expert, whereby I have power over you because you recognise that I am an expert in specific areas.

These different types have very different implications. For example, if I obey you because of coercive power then I will be unlikely to continue to obey you if you do not keep me under fairly strict surveillance. If I obey you because of expert power, then you will not need to monitor me as I accept that what you say is right. These two examples also highlight the importance of perceptions. I must recognise the power that you have in order to respond to it, and there must be enough inducement to make me give up other alternatives. If you are trying to coerce me to change my beliefs then you may not succeed if these beliefs are very fundamental.

Another related issue is the tactics which people can use to realise these power bases and the effects that they have. Tactics can vary in terms of a number of dimensions:[2]

- strength: tactics can be strong, as in a direct threat, or weak, as in dropping hints.
- rationality: for example, tactics can rely on rationality as in logical persuasion or can rely on emotional demands.
- laterality: tactics can be unilateral and have no concern for the other party or be more reciprocal as in discussion.

These dimensions are important both in terms of the effectiveness of the tactic and the way that the person using it is seen by other members of the group. For example, Falbo[3] observed people in discussion groups who had been primed to use different tactics. Members who used weak/rational tactics were seen much more positively than members who used strong/non-rational tactics.

How power and status are demonstrated

Some of the most interesting examples of the realities of power and status in everyday groups were published by W. F. Whyte over half a century ago.[4] He risked life and limb (or at least limb) by joining a street corner gang as a participant observer. He interviewed all the gang members and made extensive notes on interaction and communication. One specific event which highlighted the importance of the status hierarchy was the bowling match where Doc, the gang leader, showed an uncharacteristic loss of form. His score was overtaken by Alec, who had very low status. After some barracking from the other members, it came as no surprise that Alec's accuracy went on a downward spiral and Doc came through as winner.

Whyte observed another illustration of status pressures in his restaurant study where there was a conflict between the formal and informal systems. The cooks, who regarded themselves as high status, resented taking orders direct from the waitresses, who were regarded as low status. The solution to this was the invention of the spike, which became a standard feature of the fast food restaurant. The waitress wrote the customers' orders and then placed them on the metal spike by the cooking area. The cooks took the orders from the spike and dealt with them in the appropriate order. This re-established the cooks' sense of autonomy and high status as they did not have to react directly to instructions from waitresses. Having to develop this intermediate step may seem trivial or even insulting from an outsider's viewpoint but many issues of status are based around symbolic features of the situation.

Power and status and the rest

One practical and theoretical difficulty is separating out the demonstration of power from other concepts. For example, in the last chapter on leadership we used the book by Michael Shea as an example of the practitioners' view. He also has a clear view of the distinction between power and leadership:

Power suggests sanction, the ability to coerce or buy what is wanted. Modern leadership is more to do with inspiration or influence, manipulating people and getting them to follow you, making your goals and theirs the same.[5]

As leaders can also occupy formal positions of authority, it is important to assess what effects such positions can have on the potential and actual followers. And the most powerful study of this dynamic comes from Stanley Milgram.

Milgram's obedience to authority

Perhaps the most well-known (and certainly among the most controversial) series of experiments on our reaction to authority is the work of Stanley Milgram.[6] The best way of recognising the significance of these studies is to put yourself in the role of subject and predict how you would behave, as follows:

You have answered an advertisement in the local evening paper to participate in a study of learning undertaken by the very prestigious Yale University. You go to the very impressive main building and are shown to the psychological laboratory where you are met by a scientist in white coat and are introduced to another subject who has already arrived, a very pleasant middle-aged man. The scientist explains he is running an experiment on the relationship between punishment and learning and you draw lots to decide who will be the learner. You end up as the teacher and you are taken to the next room to watch the 'learner' being strapped into apparatus which looks rather like an electric chair with electrodes strapped to his wrist. The experimenter assures him that although any shocks may be extremely painful they will not cause any permanent damage.

You are briefly wired up yourself to receive a small shock (45 volts) from the apparatus so you can appreciate what is happening. Then you are taken next door and introduced to the task. You are also shown how to use the control panel which is used to signal the learner's answers and to administer any shocks. Your task is to read a list of word pairs and then go back through the list reading the first word of each pair and the four test words. The learner has to remember which of the test words was in the original pair and press the right button. Every time he makes a mistake you have to flip a switch and give him an electric shock. On the next mistake you have to flip the next switch and continue up the panel of switches which are labelled from 15 volts in 15 volt stages right up to 450 volts. The lowest switches are also labelled Slight Shock (15 to 60 volts) and the upper ones Danger: Severe Shock (375–420 volts). The last few switches are marked XXX (435–50 volts). For British readers it is worth remembering that this is four times the standard mains voltage in the USA.

After a few practice runs, the experiment begins. How far would you be prepared to go up the scale of shocks? How would you react when confronted by pounding on the wall, screams of pain and complaints of a weak heart from the subject next door? Would you be reassured by the experimenter telling you that you must go on? Decide on your reaction before you read on.

And what happened

As you may have guessed, the situation is rigged – the learner is a stooge who is not receiving shocks and is acting from a pre-determined script. None of the teachers – the real subjects – saw through this subterfuge in any of the variations that Milgram carried out – they all thought they were in a real situation.

In the first run of the experiment, there were no sounds from the learner except for a pounding on the wall at 300 and 315 volts. After 315 volts, the learner made no further attempts to answer and there was no further pounding.

Subjects who refused to continue with the experiment often showed extreme tension, as the following quote suggests, coming from a subject who did refuse to continue:

> He's banging in there. I'm gonna chicken out. I'd like to continue, but I can't do that to a man . . .. I'm sorry I can't do that to a man. I'll hurt his heart. You take your check . . .. No really, I couldn't do it.[7]

And consider the behaviour of a subject who carried on:

> I observed a mature and initially poised businessman enter the laboratory smiling and confident. Within twenty minutes he was reduced to a twitching, stuttering wreck, who was rapidly approaching a point of nervous collapse. He constantly pulled on his earlobe, and twisted his hands. At one point he pushed his fist into his forehead and muttered: 'Oh, God, let's stop it.' And

yet he continued to respond to every word of the experimenter, and obeyed to the end.[8]

The series of experiments

Milgram did a series of experiments – nineteen in all to test variations in the situation experienced by the real subjects. From experiment 5, there was a revised schedule of protests from the learner. This included:

- groans of pain and discomfort which started at 75 volts and were regularly repeated up to 300 volts.
- mention of pain and heart trouble at 195 volts: 'Ugh! Let me out of here! Let me out of here! My heart's bothering me. Let me out of here! You have no right to keep me here! Let me out! Let me out of here! Let me out! Let me out of here! My heart's bothering me. Let me out! Let me out!'
- regular requests to 'Get me out of here!'
- shouting and screaming, especially after 270 volts.
- the final dramatic plea at 330 volts: (Intense and prolonged agonised scream) 'Let me out of here! Let me out of here! My heart's bothering me. Let me out, I tell you! (Hysterically) Let me out of here! Let me out of here! You have no right to hold me here. Let me out! Let me out! Let me out! Let me out of here! Let me out! Let me out!'

Despite this modification there was no change to the pattern of results.

Milgram's research received tremendous publicity, partly because of the dramatic results, and partly because it raised serious ethical questions. In his main book, Milgram included a lengthy appendix which discussed ethical considerations and responded to critics like Diana Baumrind who questioned 'the kind of indignity to which Milgram's subjects were exposed'.[9] You can make up your own mind about the appropriateness of these experiments but it is worth emphasising the careful way that Milgram monitored and debriefed his subjects.

Factors influencing compliance

The profile of results across the nineteen experiments revealed that there were specific factors which influenced compliance:

- closeness of victim: the closer the victim the lesser the compliance
- closeness of experimenter: the more active the surveillance done by the experimenter, the more the compliance
- influence of the setting; the higher the prestige or status of the setting, the more compliance
- group pressure: the actions of a group of 'stooge' subjects could either increase or decrease compliance depending on the direction of the group actions

Reflections on Milgram

It is worth emphasising a number of important features of the Milgram study. The subjects were 'normal' people; Milgram was especially careful to ensure that there was no possibility of the results being attributed to 'cruel' or 'sick' subjects. He also repeated the study on men and women: both sexes showed similar results.

One feature which is not often considered is the speed of the situation. As the learning task is so quick, it does not take long before subjects can reach the top of the scale of the shocks. Would subjects have responded any differently if they had more time to consider their actions?

Especially important for the theme of this book are the small group variations which Milgram used which showed how the actions of others affected individuals.

One final speculation is what would happen now if the experiment were repeated? The ethical constraints which psychologists now work under mean that it is most unlikely that the experiment could be repeated in its original form. Would the subjects of the 1990s behave any differently?

Milgram's explanation

Milgram concluded that his subjects had entered what he called the 'agentic' state, whereby they abdicated their individual sense of responsibility and became an agent of the experimenter. This is analogous in some ways to the idea of deindividuation which will be discussed in Chapter 9.

One discussion which followed the publication of Milgram's findings was how far we can generalise the findings from this study, as in his own comparison with atrocities such as the My Lai massacre in Vietnam where the soldiers' defence for the slaughter of innocent villagers was that they were following orders.

Liking

After considering the significance of the Milgram situation, it is perhaps welcome relief to think about the fact that people in groups do like one another. However, this liking is never or rarely evenly distributed within the group; as with status relationships, some members have more than others.

One useful approach to the study of liking patterns in groups is known as sociometry and was originated many years ago by Jacob Moreno.[10] He charted the relationships between members in groups (sociograms) and investigated the implications of different patterns. Again take a group that you are familiar with and chart the positive relationships between the members – what are the consequences of these patterns?

A

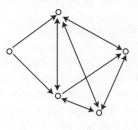

B

C

Figure 4

Figure 4 gives three examples of small group sociograms with very different dynamics:

- group A has a 'star' who will be critical to the well-being of the group
- group B has an 'isolate' figure who will either drop out or cause some disruption if he/she tries to get involved in the group interaction
- group C have a mutual trio and there is the danger of them becoming a clique and isolating other members. Alternatively, the other members may form an alliance and create an intergroup.

The search for group roles

Until recently, the typical description of roles in small groups borrowed the three-way distinction originally set out by Benne and Sheats:[11]

- group task roles, such as initiating ideas, requesting or giving information
- group maintenance roles, such as supporting or encouraging others, or resolving tension
- individual roles, such as blocker or recognition-seeker

This description does beg some important questions. It seems to mix up descriptions of behaviour (as in information-giving) and broader clusters of behaviour which are more like what we usually class as roles (as in the individual roles, which are all negative). For these reasons, I shall focus on more recent attempts to investigate roles in groups which have suggested a much more complex organisation and interrelationship of member role preferences and group effectiveness. So we shall investigate in some detail one of the leading examples of this approach: Belbin's team roles.

R. M. Belbin and team roles

The foreword to Meredith Belbin's first major text on management teams suggests that it is 'the most important single contribution of the past decade to our understanding of how human organisations work' on the grounds that the management team is critical to the success of every organisation and that our 'knowledge of what makes a successful team is tiny'[12] Of course, nearly twenty years after this was written, there is now much more research on team dynamics. But Belbin's work still demands special attention as it was derived from many years' systematic observation of groups and still provides one of the most accessible and comprehensive analyses of team roles which can be applied to a range of groups.

Over a period of around ten years, Belbin and colleagues observed several hundred teams of managers engaged in management games and exercises, using an observation scheme which was developed from Bales's IPA discussed in Chapter 3. They administered questionnaires and personality tests and manipulated the membership of the teams to see how successful different combinations were. The result of this research was a comprehensive model of team-building which is based on the following observations:

- that the behaviours of team members are organised in a limited number of team roles which are independent of the members' technical expertise or formal status
- that managers tend to consistently adopt one or two of these team roles
- that these preferred team roles are linked to personality characteristics
- that the effectiveness of the team depends upon the combination of team roles adopted by the team members

One of the best ways of evaluating Belbin's theory is to try it for yourself. His questionnaire is printed at the back of the book.[13] There is advice on how to interpret high and low scores although there are only limited norms given for comparison. Check your profile and read on.

The team roles

Belbin identifies eight team roles and their main contribution to the group is given in Table 19. He also links each role strongly to a given personality type which I have not reproduced here as I think it implies too static a picture of team dynamics.

The titles in brackets are the labels used in Belbin's earlier book. He renamed roles mainly because managers using the system felt that the original labels were inappropriate in some ways. For example, chair was considered too sexist and also to imply too high a status. So chair became co-ordinator. Company worker was considered to have

Table 19

Role	Main contribution to the group
Co-ordinator (chair)	Organises and co-ordinates Keeps team focused on main objectives Keeps other members involved
Team leader (shaper)	Initiates and leads from the front Challenges complacency or ineffectiveness Pushes and drives towards the goal
Innovator (plant)	Provides new and creative ideas
Monitor-evaluator	Provides dispassionate criticism
Team worker	Promotes good team spirit
Completer	Checks things are completed Monitors progress against deadlines
Implementer (company worker)	Practical and hard-working Focuses on the practical nitty-gritty
Resource investigator	Makes contacts outside the group

rather negative connotations and to be too low in status, and so it became implementer.[14]

Some implications/observations

Perhaps the most fundamental implication of this approach is that all roles are valuable, unlike other approaches which suggest that some roles are destructive or negative. However, my own experience in using the questionnaire is that, even with the revised titles, individuals do feel that some roles are considerably more 'attractive' than others. People feel pleased to be identified as a plant but not so satisfied at being an implementer.

Another major implication is the suggestion that groups can develop strategies to adjust any perceived imbalance. For example, one of the illustrations Belbin uses in his first book is the management team who discovered after doing the questionnaire that they were all strong shapers. They realised that, left to their natural devices, they would all be pushing so hard to support their own points of view that the group would never achieve anything and be locked in perpetual conflict. As a result, they worked out a number of strategies which they used successfully to make the most of their creative energies and minimise the chances of disruptive conflict. They elected the cleverest person as the plant. He was then allowed to select the chair on the basis that a good, compatible chair/plant combination is often associated with success. The plant was sent off to think at regular intervals which allowed the other members to get on with business. They also adopted very clear decision-making rules which avoided lengthy argument, voting on every issue.

Another important implication is best expressed as a question – using Belbin's role descriptions, who is the leader? Is it the chair or the shaper or is this another notion of dual leadership along the task/social lines we met in Chapter 6. Belbins's answer to this is that it depends on the situation: 'just as there are horses for courses, so there are leaders for teams'.[15] Where the situation demands both 'skilful use of the reserves of the group with the effective control of team members' then the strong chair is the most effective leader. Where the situation needs someone to instigate action and drag the team along with them then the shaper is more effective. Deciding what the situation requires needs a detailed knowledge of the team members and the job or tasks facing them. Belbin also suggests that a tougher and more intelligent chair can provide effective leadership to the Apollo or think-tank type of group discussed below.

Belbin's recipe for success

Based on his observations of successful teams over the years, Belbin offers a recipe for an effective team which is a combination of the following qualities:

The right person in the chair

This means that the person who is carrying out the functions of chairing the group meetings has the appropriate personality and skills, i.e. they are trusted by the other members and know how to control the discussion without dominating it.

One strong plant in the group

By a strong plant, Belbin means someone who is both creative and clever and who has the right types of creativity and interests for the task in hand.

Fair spread in mental abilities

The good news for us lesser mortals is that a group composed completely of very clever people often if not invariably fails as a team (what Belbin christened the Apollo syndrome). Such a group spends so much time analysing and criticising each other's ideas that they do not achieve much. What is needed is a spread of abilities, including the clever plant and competent chair.

Wide team-role coverage

This increases the range of the team and can also mean that there is no unnecessary friction in which different members 'compete' for the same role.

Good match between attributes and responsibilities

This is where members are given roles and jobs which fit their abilities and personal characteristics.

Adjustment to realisation of imbalance

Like the group of shapers who adjusted a few paragraphs ago, this is where the group can recognise any gaps in its make-up and can adopt strategies to make good these problems.

How far can we generalise Belbin's results?

There are a number of important issues which need to be resolved before we can confidently apply Belbin's results to every group everywhere:

Are the behaviour descriptions valid?

Can we be happy that the descriptions of behaviour used by Belbin accurately capture the essential features of team roles? My conclusion (supported by my own observations of teams and groups) is that he does offer valid summaries of consistent patterns of behaviour in groups. Unfortunately there is not yet enough independent research on Belbin's system to provide categorical support.[16]

Does Belbin's questionnaire give a reliable measure of the roles?

Despite the age and extensive use of the questionnaire, there seems to be surprisingly little work on its reliability and validity, apart from Belbin's own research. Adrian Furnham and colleagues searched the Social Science Citation Index from 1982 to 1992 and found no studies at all. They then conducted their own analysis and suggested that 'there remains some doubt, from a psychometric point of view, whether he has been able to provide a reliable measure of these role preferences'.[17] Unfortunately they did not use the standard method of scoring and were immediately criticised by Belbin who now uses Interplace, a computer-based system which integrates self-reports and observations. This system is only available on a commercial basis.[18] But, of course, this does not allay possible doubts over the orginal questionnaire.

However, more recently, Victor Dulewicz[19] has done further statistical analysis on managers' scores on both Belbin's role and the associated personality profiles. When these scores were correlated with bosses' ratings of managers' performances, he found that the results were in line with the role descriptions offered by Belbin's ratings which confirms that the role preferences seem to be both valid and reliable measures. Dulewicz's paper also provides a good summary of the roles and how they were developed.

Weren't Belbin's studies done on limited samples and in a limited context?

The immediate answer to this has to be yes. For example, in the research discussed in the first book, Belbin notes that the management teams were predominantly male and from a very limited range of ethnic backgrounds. Similarly, there was a possible limited mix of social and cultural backgrounds. Without much more comprehensive information on different types and compositions of groups we must be wary of over-generalising.

What are the consequences of labelling?

Belbin recommends that groups should complete the questionnaire and then discuss their respective profiles. This means that each member will be 'labelled' with their results. Everyone in the group will know their own profile and everyone else's. But what are the psychological consequences of this process? How does this new self-knowledge affect you and others? This does not seem to have been investigated as yet (and it is also very difficult to investigate). Suppose you do the Belbin questionnaire and come out as a strong plant – what does this do to your self-image and expectations? It could make you over-confident in your own creative abilities. What if the rest of the team come to rely on you to provide all the ideas? Will this more 'pressurised' situation feel the same as before?

What if your perceptions do not match others' perceptions of you?

Belbin discusses this problem in his second book. On the basis of work he has done comparing self and other perceptions, he suggests that when individuals complete his questionnaire they can end up with one of three profiles:

- coherent, where the individual's profile matches the perceptions of others
- discordant, where there is a mismatch. The individual's perception directly conflicts with the perceptions of others. In this case, individuals need to take action either by reassessing their self-conception or by reconsidering how they project themselves to others
- confused, where there is also a mismatch but it is inconsistent both with self and others' perceptions. In this case, individuals need to reconsider what roles they wish to take on in groups

So can you trust your score?

Given the questions raised above, if you do the Belbin questionnaire, the obvious answer is to check any results by discussing your profile with friends who know how you operate in groups and who you can trust to give an honest summary of your strengths and weaknesses. You may also like to talk to people who see you in very different groups to see if the same picture emerges.

Alternatives to Belbin

This chapter has focused on Belbin as his work is both accessible and widely used. There are other schemes which also suggest that group effectiveness is based upon successful co-ordination of specific member roles.

One well-known system in the UK has been developed by Margerison and McCann.[20] This Team Management System (TMS) offers a range of tools and methods including a questionnaire designed to measure individual work preferences on dimensions such as decision-making and relationships, and an analysis of the functional demands of given work roles. They also define the eight key roles for an effective team in ways which invite comparison with Belbin. At least some of these roles share common attributes: Belbin's 'shaper' seems similar to the TMS role 'thruster organiser', Belbin's 'plant' seems similar to TMS 'creator innovator'. TMS provides managers who complete their questionnaire with a report which identifies their preferred roles. There are also important differences from Belbin – teams must be properly coordinated and they identify a set of skills known as 'linking skills' which can be used by all the team members.

As with Belbin, TMS offer examples and evidence which suggest that organisations have used the scheme effectively. To date, there does not seem to have been an independent comparison of the two systems in terms of their relative usefulness.

Communication and structure

As the previous sections have shown, communication and structure are irretrievably interlinked. You can recognise the structure of the group by charting the communication, and the communication creates and maintains the structure. For example, various studies have shown that about two-thirds of the communication in a group will be upward, i.e. from the less powerful to the more powerful members. There have also been attempts to explain this pattern of communication in terms of the power distance between the members.[21]

One influential set of experiments which have claimed to show important relationships between communication, structure and group output are the network experiments.

The network experiments

This set of experiments and generalisations is reviewed in many social science textbooks on group interaction.[22] The work has

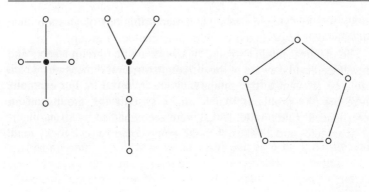

Centralised networks   Decentralised networks

Figure 5

generated a number of findings which have been generally accepted. For example, it seems that centralised networks are more efficient than decentralised networks on simple tasks when the member at the centre or hub is able to pull information together in an effective way. As this central member can be overloaded, it also appears that decentralised networks are much more efficient than centralised networks when tasks become more complex. Examples of centralised and decentralised networks are given in Figure 5.

Unfortunately these studies are a very good example of an experimental design which is so controlled that it is very unlikely that we can automatically apply these findings to real face-to-face groups. No channels are ever completely closed in real groups given that we can communicate both verbally and nonverbally. It is also seldom true in everyday groups that all members need to participate in order to solve the task. Finally, the network experiments do not allow the participants to change the structure of the network over time, which again can be achieved by everyday groups.

Integrating the structures

One unfortunate aspect of the work we have reviewed in this chapter is that the different strands have been undertaken in relative isolation from one another. As a result we do not have an integrated picture of how the different dimensions of structure relate to one another. For example, how does liking interrelate with status or role preference to detemine whether the contributions of an individual member will be accepted by other members of a group?

The practical implications of this work are that group leaders and members must be aware of the different structural dimensions which could be relevant to the groups they are involved in. For example, there are the problems which might arise if the group had an 'unbalanced' role profile. If that were accompanied by strong interpersonal likes and dislikes, then the group could be on a rocky road.

Notes

1 This classification was proposed by French and Raven and has become well accepted: French, J. R. P. and Raven, B. (1959) The base of social power. In Cartwright, D. (ed.) *Studies in Social Power*. Ann Arbor, MI: Institute for Social Research.

2 See pages 178ff. of: Wilke, H. A. M. and Meertens, R. W. (1995) *Group Performance*. London: Routledge.

3 This study was reported in 1977 by Falbo: Falbo, T. (1977) The multidimensional scaling of power strategies. *Journal of Personality and Social Psychology*, 35, 537–48.

4 The work of Whyte is still worth reading: Whyte, W. F. (1943) *Street Corner Society*. New York: McGraw-Hill. Whyte, W. F. (1948) *Human Relations in the Restaurant Industry*. New York: McGraw-Hill.

5 See: Shea, M. (1999) *Leadership Rules*. London: Century, page 21.

6 Milgram discusses both the studies and their implications in his classic text: Milgram, S. (1974) *Obedience and Authority*. London: Tavistock.

7 See Milgram, p. 32, note 6.

8 See Milgram, p. 377, note 6.

9 See the article by: Baumrind, D. (1964) Some thoughts on ethics of research: After reading Milgram's 'Behavioural Study of Obedience'. *American Psychologist*, 19, 421–3.

10 For an introduction to his work, see: Moreno, J. L. (1957) *The First Book on Group Psychotherapy*. New York: Beacon House.

11 The orginal specification was in the 1948 article: Benne, K. D. and Sheats, P. (1948) Functional roles of group Members. *Journal of Social Issues*, 4, 41–9.

12 The foreword by Antony Jay introduced Belbin's first major book on team roles: Belbin, R. M. (1981) *Management Teams: Why they succeed or fail*. Oxford: Heinemann.

13 See pages 153–8 at the back of Belbin's book, note 12.

14 These changes and other problems of terminology are discussed in his second book: Belbin, R. M. (1993) *Team Roles at Work*. Oxford: Butterworth Heinemann.

15 See page 62 of Belbin's second book, note 14.

16 Some interesting studies are now emerging, for example: Senior, B. (1995) Team roles and team performance: Is there really a link? Paper

presented to the Annual Conference of the Occupational Division and Section, University of Warwick.

17 You will need a fairly sophisticated understanding of statistics to follow the debate between Belbin and his critics. The quote is from page 256 of the Journal: Furnham, A., Steele, H. and Pendleton, D. (1993) A psychometric assessment of the Belbin Team-Role Self-Perception Inventory. *Journal of Occupational and Organizational Psychology*, 66, 245–57; Belbin, R.M. (1993) A reply to the Belbin Team-Role Self-Perception Inventory by Furnham, Steele and Pendleton. *Journal of Occupational and Organizational Psychology*, 66, 259–60; Furnham, A., Steele, H. and Pendleton, D. (1993) A response to Dr Belbin's reply. *Journal of Occupational and Organizational Psychology*, 66, 261.

18 Interplace is described in: Belbin Associates (1988) Interplace: Matching people to jobs. Cambridge.

19 Again you will need statistical knowledge to follow the detail in Dulewicz's paper: Dulewicz, V. (1995) A validation of Belbin's team roles from 16 PF and OPQ using bosses' ratings of competence. *Journal of Occupational and Organizational Psychology*, 68, 81–99.

20 For details of the TMS approach, see: McCann, R. and Margerison, C. (1989) Managing high-performance teams. *Training and Development Journal*, 11, 53–60.

21 See in: Wilke, H. A. M. and Meertens, R. W. (1994) *Group Performance*. London: Routledge.

22 See pages 246ff. of: Hogg, M. A. and Vaughan, G. M. (1995) *Social Psychology: An introduction*. Hemel Hempstead: Prentice Hall.

Chapter 8

And the answer is . . . group problem-solving and decision-making?

This chapter identifies major factors which influence the effectiveness of groups when they have to solve problems and/or make decisions.

I start with some examples where you are asked to speculate on the effectiveness of specific groups and then I discuss the research on which the examples are based. Using one of the main models of group process and productivity, this leads to an analysis of the main factors: the nature of the task; logical and perceptual barriers; and procedures and methods.

This leads to the question of how groups can ensure that they are operating as effectively as possible. Many procedures have been recommended as 'the best way' for problem-solving groups to behave and these are briefly reviewed.

The chapter then shows what happens when these procedures are neglected and analyses some of the most dramatic processes which have been suggested as the cause of disastrous decision-making, such as risky shift and groupthink. This raises the question of whether these are isolated phenomena which will only occur in exceptional circumstances, or whether we should all be looking out for them in all the groups we join.

Finally, the chapter summarises general principles which groups can use to review their decision-making and make practical improvements.

How do you decide?

The following examples will give you some ideas of how you react to decision-making procedures in groups and also highlight some of the main issues:

Example 1: Are you ready for consensus?

You are the leader of a group which has been asked to make an important decision which everyone in the group will feel committed to. So you need a consensus. How are you going to ensure that this is achieved?

Naturally you rush to the bookshelves and look up rules and guidelines for effective decision-making by consensus. You find the following suggestions:

- avoid arguing for your own rankings; present your position as lucidly and as clearly as possible
- avoid 'win-lose' statements in the discussion of rankings, discard the notion that someone must win and someone must lose
- avoid changing your mind only to avoid conflict and to reach agreement and harmony
- avoid conflict-reducing tendencies such as majority votes, averaging, bargaining and the like
- view differences in opinion as both natural and helpful rather than as a hindrance to decision-making
- view initial agreement as suspect – explore the reasons underlying apparent agreements

You decide to implement these rules and take these suggestions to the meeting. Assuming that the group agree to follow the rules, how will you enforce them? Can you rely on everyone to follow them simply by reading them or do you need some practice or training with them? What do you do if you feel that one or more members are not following the rules? For example, if someone changes their mind, how will you be satisfied that they have done so because they have been genuinely convinced by the arguments rather than giving in to group pressure?

What have you done?

What you have done is to adopt the rules of consensus first proposed by Hall and Watson in 1970.[1] They compared the decisions of groups who had received the instructions above with groups who were left to their own devices, having predicted that instructed groups would produce better quality decisions; make more effective use of resources; achieve more creativity as revealed by emergent solutions; and perform at a higher level than the most skilled member. Their results confirmed all predictions, except for the second. The instructed groups were superior and more innovative in their solutions, and this was attributed to the fact that the procedure 'institutionalised' any conflict.

Can we accept these conclusions?

There are many studies which have investigated how groups can achieve consensus using rules like the ones advocated by Hall and Watson. Although some endorse their conclusions, we can also find contrary evidence and problems which bedevil all investigations of group problem-solving techniques – as in the discussion of brainstorming in Chapter 1:[2]

- What do we compare?
  Consensus decisions do seem to be better than the decisions of the average member of the group but may not be any better than the decision of the most expert individual in the group.
- Are the studies representative?
  Many studies have used logical puzzles and temporary groups. So we are not looking at situations where the decisions really matter to the members or where the members matter to each other.
- Did the groups really follow the rules?
  There is always the problem of guaranteeing that the groups 'really' followed the rules in question.

Example 2: Which jury would you choose?

It has not been your day – you have just been arrested by police on suspicion of a crime which you did not commit. Your boss was attacked on his way home by a single masked assailant whom your boss did not recognise but physically resembled you. This happened to be the night of the day when you had a blazing row with the boss in front of several witnesses. Harsh words were spoken and at one point you threatened to 'fix him good and proper'. As you stayed at home alone watching television on the night in question, you do not have a convincing alibi. When the authorities decide there is enough circumstantial evidence against you to prosecute, which of the following two juries would you like to confront: A or B?

How jury A works

This jury has been described as 'evidence-driven'. They start by pooling all the information they have heard in court and decide upon an agreed account of events. They then reconsider the judge's instructions and make sure that they understand everything he said to them in his or her summing-up. They then arrive at their agreed verdict.

How jury B works

This jury has been described as 'verdict-driven'. They start by asking all the members their preferred verdict. Once the members have stated preferences, they negotiate to support or refute the majority verdict, perhaps along the lines of the classic 1957 Henry Fonda film *Twelve Angry Men*. This film is still well worth watching, not only as superb drama, but also as a fictionalised account of group decision-making processes.

Your best option?

These two model juries are based on research into how real juries work together to arrive at a verdict. Model A is much more systematic and logical. If you are genuinely innocent and the evidence is not convincing, then you should be safe with jury A.

The problem with Model B is the increased possibility of members' opinions being swayed by emotional reactions, prejudices or group pressures (back to Henry Fonda again). If you do not create a good first impression with jury B then the quality of the evidence may not be a deciding factor.

This variation in decision-making procedures is only one of a range of variables which can affect the way juries make decisions. There is now a range of research which shows how juries can be affected by a range of biases, including favouring 'attractive' defendants and operating racial and discriminatory stereotypes.[3]

Considering the importance of the decisions that juries take, this research is worrying. My own experience of being a juror made me feel even more worried about the potential group pressures in this situation. The formality of the British court is perhaps well-known from media images but these images cannot convey the emotional experience of being on the jury. You are surrounded by the trappings of tradition and authority; you are continually reminded of the responsibility residing with you and the other people you have just met; you have to negotiate a role with eleven other strangers; you feel some pressure to reach a verdict as efficiently as possible, if only from some of the other jurors who mention how being in the court is costing them precious time away from their livelihood. And there are doubtless other uncertainties and anxieties around the jury room. These anxieties can place significant pressure on the foreman of the jury who is placed in this leadership position (or is pushed into it). Will he/she have the skills and confidence to take the group past forming? And at what point in the group's development will the decision emerge?

Example 3: How well will your team pull?

You are in charge of your local tug-of-war team which is just about to face the highlight of its summer season – the match with the Warburton Warriors – your closest rivals for the regional trophy. You have obtained intelligence information that the Warriors have been practising by measuring their strength on a dynamometer and have achieved a maximum pull of about 450kg. You instruct your seven team members to go down to the gym to test themselves. They do so individually and discover that they average a pull of around 85kg. As 7 times 85 = 595, can you relax in the knowledge that your team will pull off a comfortable victory?

Unfortunately, you cannot relax – you have neglected the so-called Ringelmann effect – the finding that there is an inverse relationship between the number of people and individual performance on tasks like this. In other words, the more people you have, the less you will get out of each individual. On your next trip to the library, you come across research which suggests that you can only expect your team to achieve around 450kg.[4] What will you do? How will you motivate your members to develop that decisive push to make the difference?

How productive can groups be?

Example 3 above raises the problem that groups may not perform as well as you would expect by adding up individual performance. How can we explain this 'deficit'? Consider the following model[5]

which suggests that group performance is determined by three
factors:

- Task demands: the requirements of the task – are you being asked
  to make something, do something or arrive at a decision?
- Resources: these are the materials, equipment and skills you have
  at your disposal.
- Process: this is the method(s) or procedure(s) you use to tackle
  the task.

An example may make this clearer. Suppose you are a member of a
seven person group who have been asked to build a paper bridge
between two chairs a few feet apart. The final product of your efforts
must be capable of supporting a given weight. This task is typical of
the practical problem-solving exercises used on many management
training courses.

Resources in this situation would include the paper, scissors,
paper clips etc. which the organisers supply, as well as any specific
skills which your group members possess. Having a civil engineer
or an origami expert as members of the group can be useful in
situations like this. The process is the method you adopt. For
example, if one member is a civil engineer, you could let her
come up with the design and then everyone else co-operates to
make it; if you do not have any specialist technical expertise, are
you going to split the group into sub-groups and ask each sub-group
to come up with a design or are you going to keep the group
together?

Types of task

Another important aspect of this model is the classification of
different types of task. Again we can think of three main ways of
classifying tasks:

- Divisible or unitary?
  Can the task be divided into subtasks (divisible) or not (unitary)?
- Maximising or optimising?
  Does the group need to produce as much as possible (maximis-
  ing) or are you trying to achieve some predetermined standard
  (optimising)?
- How can the group members combine?
  There are a number of alternatives here: is the task additive,

where you add together all the members' contributions as in brainstorming? Is the task disjunctive, where the group must decide on an either-or basis between alternatives? Is the task conjunctive, where everyone must complete it? Or is the task discretionary where the group can decide how they would like to complete the task?

The type of task will be a major influence on group performance and groups should employ strategies which fit the task. For example, the best strategy on a disjunctive task is to work out which member is most expert and go along with their judgement, a strategy well-known to successful quiz teams. The best strategy on an additive task is to ensure that each member works as hard they can and to ensure that all their efforts are well co-ordinated. For example, in the tug-of-war team in example 3, you need to encourage and motivate everyone but also to make sure that the team pulls are well-timed so that individuals do not cancel out or disrupt each other's efforts.

Combining the factors

This model suggests that the performance or productivity of the group results from how the three main factors combine. We can then distinguish between actual and potential productivity:

> Actual productivity = Potential Productivity minus losses due to faulty process.[6]

This implies that groups can never surpass their potential which is an assumption that can be (and has been) challenged, especially when it comes to creative performance.[7] There are a number of assumptions in the model which could be questioned in real situations:

- The model assumes that resources are static.
  In other words, it assumes that the group is stuck with the resources it starts with. This may not be true. For example, individuals may develop confidence within the group situation so that their contribution becomes enhanced.
- The model also assumes fixed task demands.
  What if the team members realise during the course of the process that they are really in competition with another group?

This brings in all the complexities of intergroup behaviour which are discussed in the next chapter.
- The model assumes that group process must always have a negative effect.

Steiner does not concede that the group might be able to improve on its potential and we challenge this later.

However, the model does concentrate our attention on the problems of 'faulty process'[8] and this is our next stop.

Why and how can group performance be 'brought down'?

We can summarise some of the major problems using the model outlined in Table 20.

Many of these issues have already been discussed in other chapters, for example issues of normative influence in Chapter 5. Others have not and they need further explanation.

Table 20

Task problems	Resource problems	Process problems
Nature of task not clearly identified	Material and equipment not sufficient	Group approach does not match type of task
Vague or indefinite criteria of success	Member skills not sufficient	Problem-solving barriers, inappropriate influence such as conformity pressures Inappropriate team structure

Problem-solving barriers, biases and traps

Human beings do not always solve problems in a rational way – they are susceptible to a range of biases and traps, both individually and collectively. To illustrate some of the most important of these, try to answer the following questions before you read on:

- An unbiased coin is tossed three times and lands on heads each time. You have £100 to bet on the next choice – what is your bet?

- Are you more likely to be killed in the USA by shark attack or falling aeroplane parts?
- If you have read about the near nuclear meltdown which took place at Three Mile Island, does that make you more or less confident about the safety of nuclear power?
- How wide would you have to build a cube-sized tank to hold all the human blood in the world?
- How thick would a piece of standard writing paper be if you folded it in on itself 100 times?

Your answers to these questions may well illustrate your suscept-ibility to common biases in problem-solving:[9]

We may perceive selectively.

Human beings tend to perceive selectively as in the old adage – 'we see what we want to see'. When a range of scientists were asked about the Three Mile Island disaster, they interpreted the event in terms of their pre-existing attitudes. Opponents of nuclear power saw it as more evidence of the dangers involved; supporters saw it as evidence for the ultimate reliability of the safety measures in that the real disaster was avoided. This problem of selective perception may be especially important when scientists disagree about impor-tant issues of public health. If scientists are endorsing opposed views, how do the public decide which action to take?

We may have subconscious biases

For example, how would you solve the following problem: A father and son are out driving and have an accident. The father is killed outright but the son is rushed to hospital in critical condition and prepared for an operation. The surgeon comes in to operate, sees the patient and exclaims, 'I can't operate; that's my son.' How is this possible?[10]

We are very sensitive to contextual influences

An example here would be the way we can be swayed by the framing of a problem or question. If you had just seen a traffic accident and were asked how fast the cars were going when they contacted, would it make any difference if the word 'contacted' was replaced by other alternatives like bumped, collided, or smashed which suggest more or less serious impact? Research along these lines showed that the word, smashed, did have a major effect on how observers responded, increasing their estimates of speed by around 10 miles per hour. They were also influenced to report on broken glass even though this had not been part of the accident.[11]

We sometimes use inappropriate heuristics

A heuristic is a general rule of thumb. When people are confronted with complicated decisions, they can often resort to heuristics which can lead to predictable biases and inconsistencies.

For example, the representativeness heuristic suggests that what we have seen is likely to be representative of a broader range of events. Reconsider the unbiased coin tossed three times. Each time it lands heads up. If you had £100 to bet on the next toss, what would you bet? Although the actual odds are 50/50 for heads or tails, a disproportionate number of people will opt for tails on the grounds that the run must balance out.

The probability heuristic works out probability by relating it to the ease with which events can be brought to mind. For example, how did you decide which is the most likely cause of death in the USA between being killed by falling aeroplane parts or a shark? Most people have an image of shark attacks – they receive more publicity and haven't we all seen *Jaws*? So most people select shark attacks although the statistics show they are thirty times less likely than being hit by bits of loose aeroplane.

We use misleading frames of reference

One example here is what is known as anchoring, the tendency to relate a problem to an initial starting value which gives a misleading impression. For example, consider the last two problems above: the cube-shaped tank, and the folded paper.

In both cases, many people give very poor estimates because they anchor their estimate to a misleading initial image – the first few folds of paper are very small, the population of the world is very large. So we can be influenced by background information which can give a misleading impression of the scale or extent of a problem. For example, thinking about the container for the human blood, you may well have been swayed by the enormous size of the world population (estimated at 5 billion people) rather than the small amount of blood we all carry (averaging one gallon each). The estimated answer on these figures is only 870 feet. The folding paper problem works the opposite way: based on a piece of paper 0.1 millimetre thick, the answer in kilometres is around 1.27×10^{23}, which is huge by any standards.

We can fall into problem traps

Examples of traps are:

- Overconfidence, which is usually inversely related to accuracy. The more confident people are, the more likely that they are wrong!
- Self-fulfilling prophecies.
- Behavioural traps.
  An interesting example of a behavioural trap is an investment trap, where you have invested so much in a project that you are unwilling to give it up, even in the face of overwhelming evidence that it is now no longer viable.

Restating the importance of communication and interaction

One important implication in the model by Steiner (and there are several others along similar lines) is that group interaction and communication are only significant in that they contribute to 'faulty process'. In other words, they do not have any real role in *enhancing* group achievement. But can this be partly as a result of the type of studies involved?[12]

For example, earlier we noted the common finding that an interacting group will typically out-perform the average group member but will not exceed the performance of its best member, when this is measured solely by outcome measures of performance. But there are often exceptions. Using a typical problem-solving task, Nemiroff and King found that 72 per cent trained groups surpassed their best member whereas only 33 per cent untrained groups surpassed their best member.[13] And what if you test groups on tasks which are especially meaningful to them rather than abstract problems?

Michaelson and colleagues tested this proposition on student groups who met over the course semester.[14] The best individual was identified by individual score in class exams. The groups then came up with answers on the same questions. There was a process gain in 97 per cent of the groups, with the average gain of 8.8 per cent over best individual.

So this and other recent research has painted a rather different picture, emphasising that the quality of communication is critical on both simple and complex tasks. Some of the relationships between communication, interaction and other components of the decision-making process however are still not clear.

The importance of group goals

A range of studies have now shown that the presence and clarity of group goals has a major impact on group effectiveness.[15] Typical findings are that:

- groups working towards specific, difficult goals perform better than those groups without specific goals
- performance is related to goal difficulty: increase the level of difficulty and the performance will also increase, i.e. groups respond to challenges
- specific goals will have more effect than 'do-your-best' goals
- these generalisations work across a wide variety of situations and goals

These findings suggest practical strategies that can create the appropriate group environment: setting goals which cover all aspects of the performance, providing regular feedback on progress, encouraging communication between members, encouraging and supporting planning activities, and helping group members manage failure.

However, it is also important to note that many of these studies on goal-setting have been carried out as controlled experiments using volunteer subjects. A recent study of goal-setting in a research centre in a large multinational failed to support some of the usual findings.[16] Usually, increasing the difficulty of a goal will lead to increased performance until you approach the limits of the person's ability, when the relationship will level off. This did not happen and the researchers speculate on a number of possible reasons: the fact that the individuals were committed to multiple goals rather than just one; possible differences of interpretation in assessing the difficulties of the goals; and the long timescales involved. One practical implication of this is that organisations who employ goal-setting techniques with their employees should review the timescale between meetings to discuss progress. Another implication from this study concerns the goal-setting process. The organisation concerned did not offer any annual or refresher training in goal-setting to the managers involved, the majority of who were untrained. This process of interpersonal negotiation may not be as straightforward as organisations think, especially in organisations which use performance rating and bonus systems which do not seem to relate to one another and where the individuals affected may be suspicious or cynical of the process.

What alternatives do groups have?

Groups can choose from many different ways of approaching problems and making decisions. Again, some of these such as brainstorming have already been referred to in earlier chapters. Broadly speaking there are two main strategies which groups can use to revise their performance: adopting new procedures or changing their decision-making rules.

Adopting new procedures

Groups can adopt new procedures and there is no shortage of possible suggestions.[17] To give an idea of the range of possibilities we shall discuss four alternatives.

Structured problem-solving

One obvious possibility is to take the philosophy on which techniques like brainstorming are based and break down the problem-solving process into discrete stages. Each stage is addressed in turn in the right order. A typical order is:[18]

- describe the need
- define goals and criteria
- identify constraints
- generate alternative solutions
- evaluate alternative solutions
- select best overall solution
- implement the chosen solution
- evaluate its effectiveness

Nominal group technique

Nominal group technique (NGT) is a way of organising group decision-making to minimise issues of status or inhibition by certain members of the group. Ideally the group uses an external facilitator to work through the process which has three main stages: individuals working on their own to generate ideas; discussion of possible solutions; and private anonymous voting. The specific steps are:

- the problem is fully explained to the group
- individuals work separately to generate ideas and possible solutions
- all the ideas are recorded on a chart
- each idea is discussed, clarified and evaluated by the group
- individuals privately rank the ideas
- the group decision is the idea which achieves the highest average ranking

Delphi

This is a way of arriving at a group decision which does not involve a face-to-face meeting. It is especially useful if the group is composed of people who would find it difficult if not impossible to meet. The main stages are:

- enlisting the group
- distributing the statement of the problem to the group members and inviting them to respond
- compiling the responses
- sending out the compiled responses for further comment

These last two phases are then repeated until a consensus is reached. We have used this technique successfully on research projects which demanded that we convene a panel of experts who were unable to physically meet.

Encouraging group innovation

Michael West and colleagues[19] have carried out a number of studies on the factors which encourage team innovation. He has proposed a four-factor theory including vision, participative safety, climate for excellence and support for innovation. The group vision must be 'clearly understandable, shared and negotiated'.[20] It cannot be imposed on members. The quantity and quality of participation is critical and members must feel able to voice their ideas without risk of censorship or ridicule – the notion of psychological safety. The climate for excellence is described as 'a real commitment to achieving first-rate performance' and this will involve concentration on the task and conscious adoption of the best methods of achieving it. Support for innovation must be more than management rhetoric – there must be real support and encouragement to help develop new ideas.

These factors accurately predict whether a team will be able to produce innovative ideas and solutions and can be reliably measured using the Team Climate Inventory[21] which has been tested and used in the UK and Sweden.[22]

Changing decision-making

Consider your present strategy for making decisions – what are its advantages and disadvantages? There are numerous alternatives.

Table 21

Method	Advantage	Disadvantage
Decision by authority without discussion.	Speed.	Does not use members' expertise.
Decision by authority after discussion.	Allows everyone to express opinion.	Members may not be committed to the decision.
Decision by expert member.	Good decision if really expert.	May be difficult to identify the most expert member.
Average members' opinions.	Speed.	Members may not be committed to the decision.
Majority control.	Speed.	Minority can be alienated.
Minority control.	Can be useful if not everyone can attend.	Members may not be committed to the decision.
Consensus.	Members will be committed to the decision.	Can take a great deal of time, skill and energy.

Table 21 lists many of these and identifies one major advantage and disadvantage of each.

There are of course additional advantages and disadvantages to each.[23]

But how do you choose the 'best system'?

These is no such thing as the best system – different circumstances call for different methods. If I am talking to a group and smoke starts seeping under the door then I will adopt an autocratic leadership role and order the group to vacate. That is not the time for democratic discussion, and I've read the work by Latané *et al.* (see in Chapter 5).

There have been various studies comparing different methods but you have to be wary of over-generalising. For example, Janet Sniezek compared five types of decision techniques: consensus, Delphi, averaging individual judgements without discussion, 'dictator' and 'dialectic'.[24] The dictator technique starts with face-to-face discussion which then leads to the selection of one member whose judgement is then accepted by the group. The dialectical technique requires members to discuss any factors which might be biasing their judgements. In this comparison – a sales forecasting problem with groups of five college students – the dictator technique produced the most accurate judgements.

We do need to worry about how far we can generalise the supposed virtues of some of these alternative methods. Pavitt has gone so far as to argue that the evidence is so lacking that we have 'no firm basis for recommendation to practitioners concerning the use of formal discussion procedures for guiding real-world groups in their decision-making' although he does also admit that 'groups using formal procedures probably do make better decisions' and that members of groups using them do seem both more satisfied and more committed.[25]

Group performances to chill the spirit

It is not difficult to find examples of group performance which are so disastrous that you can scarcely believe them. This section explores some of the factors that have been researched which may suggest that the next major blunder will not be too far off into the future.

Leadership as folly

Many examples of disastrous decision-making can be seen in military history – the Charge of the Light Brigade, General Custer's last stand at the Little Big Horn and numerous others. One reason for such disasters is the quality of the leadership involved and this has been analysed by Norman Dixon who has uncovered a frightening tally of regular mistakes which have emanated from the military mind: including the tendency to underestimate the enemy; the inability to admit mistakes (blaming others and not learning from experience); not using reconnaissance and discounting warnings; passivity and procrastination; failure to take initiative and the rather unfortunate predisposition to frontal assaults. Dixon suggests that there is a personality link here with these errors being characteristic of the sort of personality which is attracted to and can do well in the military culture. As he has suggested:

> the 'constraining factor of militarism' (those rules and regulations designed to control military forces) not only encourage promotion of conforming over-obedient closed-minded people to positions of high command, but also constrained their activities when they got there.[26]

Although this may be a something of an overstatement with respect to many modern military organisations, there are still too many examples of military disasters to make us relax. Perhaps the appropriate way to conclude this section is with the last words of Union General John Sedwick as he stood before his men in 1864.

> 'Come, come! Why they couldn't hit an elephant at this dist—'.[27]

The risky shift

In 1961, James Stoner contradicted the received wisdom of the day that groups would tend to move towards more conservative decisions than those initially expressed by the individuals involved. He observed that groups would usually make more risky decisions. This astonished many psychologists and frightened a few political observers of the time who were concerned about the possible escalation of the Cold War between the Soviet Union and the USA to the point where some group of political decision-makers would feel it necessary to start the Third World War.

Stoner was presenting groups of six individuals with dilemmas where they had to reach a unanimous choice between cautious and risky decisions, having already considered the dilemma individually. The typical group decision was riskier than the average of the individuals' previous decisions, and this phenomenon became known as the risky shift.[28]

Moving to group polarisation

Although the publicity surrounding Stoner's work emphasised the risky shift process, he had also observed a shift to caution in some circumstances, where the group decision was less riskier than the average of the individuals' previous decisions.

Following up this observation in the late 1960s, Serge Moscovici and colleagues concluded that the actual group process was what he christened group polarisation – the group response will be more extreme than the average of the individuals but in the same direction as the individual tendencies.[29] So, if the individual average is on the cautious side, then the group decision will be more cautious than the average of the individual opinions. If the individual average is on the risky side, then the group decision will be more risky than the average of the individual opinions.

This has now become the accepted finding although the explanation can still be debated, as the individuals in the group will be subject to both normative and informational pressures as a result of the discussion. The explanation which seems to have most current support is that individuals are influenced to move towards what they see as the 'prototypical' group position as we discussed in Chapter 5.

Groupthink

The term 'groupthink' was coined by Irving Janis to describe:

a mode of thinking that people engage in when they are deeply involved in a cohesive in-group, when the members' strivings for unanimity override their motivation to realistically appraise alternative courses of action.[30]

After reading accounts of the catastrophic attempt by the Kennedy administration in 1961 to support an invasion of Cuba designed to overthrow Fidel Castro, Janis speculated on how such an able and intelligent group could make such a disastrous mis-calculation. How could they have accepted the proposal that a relatively poorly equipped force of around 1400 exiles could land at the Bay of Pigs, sweep past the assembled Cuban militia, well-equipped with their Russian armaments, incite the local population into spontaneous revolt, and take over the island?

Looking at other well-documented military catastrophes, Janis developed his model of groupthink which suggests that, given certain antecedent conditions, a group will develop a 'concurrence-seeking tendency'. This will lead to the symptoms of groupthink which in turn will lead to symptoms of defective decision-making:

The antecedent conditions

In his later book, Janis defined three main conditions:

- that the decision-makers are a cohesive group
- that there are what he called 'structural faults of the organisa-tion', such as the group being very insulated from outside influ-ences and the members being very similar in background and attitudes
- that there is a 'provocative situational context' involving high stress and external threats

The symptoms of groupthink

He defines eight major symptoms including the 'illusion of invulner-ability' which are of three main types:

- overestimating the group's position and rights
- rigid and closed patterns of thinking which include strong stereo-types of the other groups
- very strong pressures towards uniformity, with some members of the group acting as 'mindguards' and ensuring that everyone toes the line

The symptoms of defective decision-making

He defines seven main symptoms which include the general failure to clarify objectives, to consider alternative actions, or to develop contingency plans.

The results are poor or catastrophic decisions. Several descriptive studies have supported Janis's model to some degree.[31] Perhaps the most detailed is a study by Tetlock *et al.*[32] which examined all the historical incidents used by Janis plus a couple of more recent American examples from the Ford and Carter administrations. They found that a simpler model could predict the onset of group-think, focusing upon the structural faults in the organisation. The following features were most characteristic of groups with group-think tendencies:

- restricted information flow between the leader and members
- a leader who restricted the range of views consulted by the group
- a leader who was not open to any other points of view
- very formal communication within the group
- few open disagreements

This places emphasis back on the leader's responsibility to keep information flows open and to encourage debate and discussion.

Explaining groupthink

Although Janis offers a detailed description of the processes, his attempts to explain the phenomena have seemed less emphatic and have developed in a number of ways. His 1972 book emphasised the precondition of high group cohesiveness. In 1977, he defined group-think as concurrence-seeking behaviour with emphasis on the leader's role:

> When a directive leader announces his preference on a policy issue . . . the members of a cohesive group will tend to accept his choice somewhat uncritically as if it were equivalent to a group norm.[33]

Experimental studies have also tried to investigate the causal link between cohesiveness and concurrence-seeking, and have reported mixed results. Michael Hogg has pointed out that Janis's own interpretations have moved further away from cohesiveness and more to seeing groupthink as an outcome of individual responses to stress.[34] Stress produces coping reactions of avoidance and defence. These coping strategies lead to the symptoms of group-think: 'symptoms of groupthink are behavioural consequences of a coping pattern of defensive avoidance, which is mutually supported by the group'.[35] Hogg offers his own interpretation based upon notions of self-categorisation:

> From this perspective, groupthink represents an unremarkable group phenomenon in which defective decision-making processes are adopted because group members identify (i.e. self-categorise) very strongly with a group that either has no procedures for effective decision-making, or has norms that explicitly encourage groupthink.[36]

This line of argument suggests that once the members of a group are committed to a very strong self-categorisation as members of the group, then the high 'cohesion' which Janis observed is a parallel by-product. Hogg supports this analysis by pointing out that group cohesion can be defined in two rather different ways: as 'depersonalised' where members are loyal to the group as an entity; and in a more personal way as interpersonal liking and attraction between individual members. The evidence suggests that 'cohesion' as depersonalised social attraction is very strongly related to groupthink, whereas 'cohesion' as interpersonal attraction or friendship is not related.

Final thoughts on practice

Perhaps the one critical generalisation which comes out of this chapter is that groups do have a very wide range of choice in the way that they approach problem-solving and decision-making. Whether groups decide to take advantage of this range of choice, or even recognise its existence, is another matter.

Groups can also learn from their experience. For example, Janis also highlights ways of avoiding groupthink. He notes how the same Kennedy administration which supported the Bay of Pigs later adopted strategies to make sure that important decisions were thoroughly researched, like electing one member of the group to act as 'devil's advocate' at every meeting who had to find possible flaws in every proposal put to the meeting.

Perhaps the most appropriate final word comes from recent research which investigated the detailed impact of group communication and interaction processes on decision-making.[37] The five critical functions were as follows:

- thorough discussion of problem
- thorough examination of criteria for successful solution

- complete proposal of realistic alternative solutions
- full assessment of the positive aspects of each proposal
- full assessment of the negative aspects of each proposal

Problem-solving groups which can honestly claim to be achieving all these functions in open communication have the best chances of success.

Notes

1 For a discussion of the consensus rules and how they were derived, see: Hall, J. (1971) Decisions, decisions, decisions. *Psychology Today*, November.

2 The difficulties of comparing individual and group problem-solving are discussed alongside many of the other issues in this chapter in: Wilke, H. and Knippenberg, A. V. (1996) Group performance. In Hewstone, M., Stroebe, W. and Stephenson, G. M. (eds) *Introduction to Social Psychology*. 2nd edn. Oxford: Blackwell.

3 For further examples of studies of jury performance, see page 276ff. of Hogg and Vaughan, or Chapter 6 of Baron *et al.*: Baron, R. S., Kerr, N. L. and Miller, N. (1992) *Group Process, Group Decision, Group Action*. Buckingham: Open University Press; Hogg, M. A. and Vaughan, G. M. (1995) *Social Psychology: An introduction*. Hemel Hempstead: Prentice Hall.

4 The data used in this example is taken from work done by a French agricultural engineer called Max Ringelmann who conducted a series of experiments looking at the efficiency of various pulling techniques used in farming back in the late nineteenth century, described in Kravitz and Martin.

   This sort of work is typical of the work done in the early part of this century, comparing individual and group efforts, which gave rise to an interest in the effect of groups on the individual: Kravitz, D. A. and Martin, B. (1986) Ringelmann rediscovered: The original article. *Journal of Personality and Social Psychology*, 50, 936–41.

5 This model is from Steiner: Steiner, I. D. (1972) *Group Process and Productivity*. New York: Academic Press.

6 See note 5.

7 See the discussion in Baron *et al.*, note 3.

8 For a further discusion of research which investigates these problems, see Chapter 5 of: Brown, R. (1988) *Group Processes. Dynamics within and between groups*. Oxford: Blackwell.

9 This summary is based upon one of the best books on decision-making I have ever read in terms of both explaining the theory and showing how it can be applied to everyday problems. There is a reader's survey at the start of the book containing questions where you can test your susceptibility to some of these biases: Plous, S. (1993) *The Psychology of Judgment and Decision Making*. New York: McGraw-Hill.

10 The surgeon is of course the boy's mother. Did your mental picture of the incident fall into the stereotype trap of assuming that all surgeons are male?

11 See pages 32ff. of the book by Plous, note 9.

12 The article by Salazar not only provides a critique of the ideas put forward by Steiner but also describes studies which have tested the relationship between communication and decision quality. See also the article by Stasson and Bradshaw: Salazar, A. J. *et al.* (1994) In search of true causes: Examination of the effect of group potential and group interaction on decision performance. *Human Communication Research*, 20, 529–59; Stasson, M. F. and Bradshaw, S. D. (1995) Explanation of individual–group performance difference. What sort of bonus can be gained through group interaction? *Small Group Research*, 26, 296–308.

13 Nemiroff and King used the well-known NASA moon problem in: Nemiroff, P. M. and King, D. C. (1975) Group decision-making performances as influenced by consensus and self-orientations. *Human Relations*, 28, 1–21.

14 This study is described in: Michaelson, L. K., Watson, W. E. and Black, R. H. (1989) A realistic test of individual versus group consensus decision-making. *Journal of Applied Psychology*, 74, 834–9.

15 This article reviews major studies to date, develops a model of the relation between group goals and performance, and develops the practical recommendations summarised here: Weldon, E. and Weingart, L. R. (1993) Group goals and group performance. *British Journal of Social Psychology*, 32, 307–34.

16 See: Yearta, S. K., Maitlis, S. and Briner, R. B. (1995) An exploratory study of goal setting in theory and practice: A motivational technique that works? *Journal of Occupational and Organizational Psychology*, 68, 237–52.

17 For examples, see the suggestions in Chapter 11 of: Kayser, T. A. (1994) *Building Team Power*. Burr Ridge, IL: Irwin.

18 This presentation of the step-wise model of problem-solving is adapted from pages 5–43 of: Scholtes, P. R. *et al.* (1988) *The Team Handbook: How to use teams to improve quality*. Madison, WI: Joiner Associates.

19 The theory is fully described in the following article: West, M. A. (1990) The social psychology of innovation in groups. In West, M. A. and Farr, J. L. (eds) *Innovation and Creativity and Work. Psychological and Organizational Strategies*. Chichester: Wiley.

20 For a brief overview of this work, see the article which contains these quotes. There is also a useful checklist on page 200: Anderson, N., Hardy, G. and West, M. (1994) Innovative teams at work. In Mabey, C. and Iles, P. (eds) *Managing Learning*. London: Routledge.

21 The TCI is fully described in: Anderson, N. R. and West, M. A. (1994) *The Team Climate Inventory: Manual and user's guide*. Windsor, Berkshire: ASE Press.

22 The Team Climate Inventory has been tested on work teams in Sweden. Despite some cultural differences, it remained a valid instrument: Angrell, A. and Gustafson, G. (1994) The team climate inventory (TCI) and group innovation: A psychometric test on a Swedish sample

of work groups. *Journal of Occupational and Organizational Psychology*, 67, 143–51.

23 For a fuller version of this table, see page 238ff. in: Johnson, D. W. and Johnson, F. P. (1994) *Joining Together: Group theory and group skills*. 5th edn. Boston: Allyn and Bacon.

24 This study is also discussed in Plous (note 9): Sniezek, J. A. (1989) An examination of group process in judgemental forecasting. *International Journal of Forecasting*, 5, 171–8.

25 For a full review, see: Pavitt, C. (1993) What (little) we know about formal group discussion procedures. A review of relevant research. *Small Group Research* 24, 217–35.

26 The quote is from the recent article. His main research is described in the following book: Dixon, N. (1976) *On the Psychology of Military Incompetence*. London: Cape; Dixon, N. (1994) Disastrous decisions. *The Psychologist*, 7, 303–7.

27 For this and other examples of human fallibility, see: Peter, L. J. (1985) *Why Things Go Wrong*. Hemel Hempstead: George Allen and Unwin.

28 Stoner's original book was in 1961. For a longer summary of this work and an example of the dilemmas used by Stoner, see pages 206ff. of Pennington: Stoner, J. A. F. (1961) *A Comparison of Individual and Group Decisions Involving Risk*. Cambridge, MA: MIT; Pennington, D. C. (1986) *Essential Social Psychology*. London: Edward Arnold.

29 The original paper on group polarisation is from 1969. For a recent discussion, see page 61ff. of Wilke and Meertens: Moscovici, S. and Zavalloni, M. (1969) The group as a polariser of attitudes. *Journal of Personality and Social Psychology*, 12, 125–35; Wilke, H. A. M. and Meertens, R. W. (1994) *Group Performance*. London: Routledge.

30 Janis produced his major text on groupthink in 1972 with a second edition in 1982. The definition is from page 9 of the 1982 book: Janis, I. (1982) *Victims of Groupthink: A psychological study of foreign policy decisions and fiascos*. 2nd edn. Boston: Houghton Mifflin.

31 One suggestion has been that the Thatcher government in the UK was affected by groupthink during the Falklands War with Argentina. Many examples of anecdotes and accounts of cabinet life can be found in Hennessy. The Lord Franks report is also a rich source of material on events around that time: Franks, Lord (1983) *Falklands Island Review, report of a committee of Privy councillors*. CMND8787. London: HMSO; Hennessy, P. (1986) *Cabinet*. Oxford: Blackwell.

32 See the full study in: Tetlock, P. E., Peterson, R.S., Mcguire, C., Chang, S. and Feld, P. (1992) Assessing political group dynamics: A test of the groupthink model. *Journal of Personality and Social Psychology*, 63, 403–25.

33 See page 131 of: Janis, I. L. and Mann, L. (1977) *Decision making: A psychological analysis of conflict, choice and commitment*. New York: Free Press.

34 See page 135ff. of: Hogg, M. A. (1992) *The Social Psychology of Group Cohesiveness: From attraction to social identity*. Hemel Hempstead: Harvester. Wheatsheaf.

35 This quote comes from Janis pages 481–2 (note 30).

36 See page 135 of Hogg (note 34).
37 See: Hirokawa, R. (1988) Group communication research: Considerations for the use of interaction analysis. In Tardy, C. H. (ed.) *A Handbook for the Study of Human Communication: Methods and instruments for observing, measuring and assessing communication process.* Norwood NG: Ablex.

Chapter 9

When groups collide – enter the intergroup

This chapter investigates what often happens when two groups have to communicate across their group boundaries and relates these processes to theories and ideas from previous chapters. After a brief definition of intergroup situations, we visit four 'classic' studies of intergroup behaviour and examine how they have been explained, before looking for general principles which can account for the difficulties which often arise in intergroup situations. This leads to a discussion of how these ideas can be used to make practical suggestions for communication across group boundaries.

Defining the intergroup

One of the most widely quoted definitions of intergroup behaviour comes from Muzafer Sherif:

> Whenever individuals belonging to one group interact collectively or individually with another group or its members in terms of their group identification, we have an instance of intergroup behaviour.[1]

Using this definition it is very easy to think of obvious examples of intergroup communication:

- a negotiation between management and union representatives in a company
- a meeting between two rival gangs of teenagers outside a dance hall

As these examples suggest, intergroup communication is often associated with tension and conflict and we return to this theme later. It is also important to recognise that Sherif's definition covers much more subtle examples where the group definitions may not be so immediately obvious to the outsider. And this harks back to the distinction between personal and social identity which was introduced in Chapter 2. Wherever individuals perceive an 'in-group' of which they are a member and an 'out-group' which is different, then we can talk about an intergroup situation. For example, the village community group assembled for its annual general meeting may appear as one large group to an outside visitor but may be much more complex as experienced by the members. Suppose there are a number of 'newcomers' to the village who are anxious to get involved. They may well be perceived as a separate group by the longstanding members who will treat them with some reserve or suspicion. The newcomers may then respond to this labelling by becoming more cohesive and the intergroup becomes a powerful reality. Some of the processes which may result from this social division are illustrated in the studies which are described below.

Study 1: The Sherifs' summer camp

In the late 1940s, Muzafer Sherif was a Turkish professor living in America with an American wife. As a result of his own experiences of prejudice and discrimination, he became interested in discovering the roots and causes of this behaviour. He became dissatisfied with the explanations which were current in the literature at the time which tended to explain prejudice and discrimination in terms of individual processes. For example, one major theory suggested that discrimination against outgroups was initiated by individuals with particular personality characteristics or by individuals who were very frustrated. It had been believed for some time that frustration leads to aggression towards a convenient scapegoat.[2] Sherif was unconvinced by these explanations as they did not seem to account for the comprehensive and pervasive discrimination which he saw in the society around him. There was too much discrimination to believe it was all attributable to some 'sick' individuals.

As a result of this, he decided to set up a naturalistic experiment (to avoid any accusations of the experimental design creating the effects) which examined relationships between groups in competition to see what conflict might occur and how it might be resolved. With a group of colleagues, he took over an American summer camp – that fine American institution which is now recognised worldwide thanks to the ubiquitous Snoopy cartoons – on three separate occasions, in 1949, 1953 and 1954.[3] His team dutifully observed and investigated the activities of the participants who were unaware that they were, in fact, experimental subjects. As an example of how taken in the boys were by the reality of the experience, Sherif recounts that he met one of the boys many years later who remembered the camp in the course of conversation. He gave a detailed account of the events, blissfully unaware that he was talking to the former camp 'handyman' who had been wandering around throughout the duration of the camp.

Sherif also used this series of experiments to deliberately eliminate the factors considered important by previous theories. For example, his subjects were young boys from very similar backgrounds to eliminate any tensions due to existing social divisions. They were also thoroughly vetted to eliminate any suggestions of personal instability or frustration. In the earlier trials, the boys were allowed to mingle and develop friendships before being formally organised into groups. The formal groups were assembled so that existing friendships were split up, a device which should have encouraged positive and friendly communication between the groups, but which actually made no difference to the chain of events which ensued.

Of the three experiments, the most widely reported is the last one, usually known as the Robber's Cave Experiment, after the name of the summer camp. The Sherifs were interested in the factors which would create or maintain conflict between the groups and organised the camp in the following ways:

- the boys were split into two groups who were involved in separate activities and living accommodation to allow norms and group structures to develop
- the two groups were brought together in competitive games and other activities

In a recent recorded discussion, Carolyn Sherif described some of the background:

> Our hypothesis was that although the pre-existing differences between groups (religious differences and gender differences and so on) do contribute to the conflict, that for individuals to develop these nasty ways, it was not necessary that they have a long history. To have a realistic confrontation between those groups was a sufficient condition.[4]

There are numerous graphic accounts of the conflict which followed when the groups were brought together to compete. There were fights (which everyone agreed had been started by the other group); insults were exchanged; and the groups destroyed each other's property. In each experiment, the conflict mushroomed to an almost intolerable level and Sherif and his colleagues were hard-pressed to prevent an outbreak of serious disorder.

Typical behaviour patterns

What the summer camps demonstrated was a typical pattern of behaviour which has been demonstrated in numerous other settings and with various types of groups, including mature adults. It is also a pattern which is depressingly easy to create in a group exercise or role-play.[5] The main features of this pattern are summarised in Table 22.

This description also highlights the breakdown in communication which can lead to what has been described as autistic hostility where the circumstances generate almost automatic responses which are guaranteed to escalate the conflict.[6] The decrease in overt communication makes it even less likely that the groups will understand their respective positions. The communication that does occur is distorted to serve the needs of the conflict. The hostility also serves to establish self-fulfilling prophecies from both sides.

Another notion that seems to underpin these processes and which seems to share similar features is what has been called entrapment, where individuals or groups become over-committed to a course of action and then get stuck in a spiral of behaviour which they seem unable to escape from.[7] A simple and trivial example would be waiting for the bus when you are trying to reach an important appointment. The bus is late – how do you decide to respond? The longer you wait the more certain you become that it is 'just about to arrive'. You become more anxious. If entrapment sets in, you become more determined to wait, and so on and so on. More serious examples would include the divorce proceedings where both parties are determined to 'win their share' at whatever cost.

Various pressures seem to increase the chances of entrapment, such as the value you attach to the reward associated with achieving the goal, the presumed increased proximity to goal, and the perceived cost of giving up. Situations which are likely to invoke this

Table 22

Area	The process	What happens
Within each group	Biased perceptions	Members will develop biased perceptions which they will not necessarily be consciously aware of. They will exaggerate the value of their own efforts and be quite certain that they know the other group's position even when they do not.
	Strong task leaders emerge	Each group will choose leaders who are liable to be authoritarian and hard taskmasters.
	Cohesive, conformist culture develops	Each group will become very close-knit and conformist. It will concentrate very hard on the task in hand (usually beating the other group!).
	Runaway norms	The norms of competition will become progressively more extreme unless checked by other circumstances.
Between each group	Active discrimination	Groups will actually discriminate against one another at every available opportunity.
	Distorted communication	Exchanges between the groups are liable to be unfriendly or hostile. Messages will be misinterpreted or misunderstood.
	Escalating conflict	There is liable to be a progressive escalation of conflict.
	Stereotypic distortion	Group see each other in 'mirror image' terms: we are good and you are bad.

process are those where the participants have not set any advance limits and where withdrawal is seen to involve possible loss of face.

Trying to resolve the conflict

Having created this high level of conflict, the Sherifs took several steps to reduce it:

Social contact

For example, a party was organised so the boys could mix and enjoy themselves with no competitive overtones. In fact, both groups seized upon this opportunity to continue the battle. Cakes and sandwiches make good missiles!

Common enemy

The camp was challenged by another camp at baseball. Boys from both groups were chosen in the camp side. Hostilities were suspended, but only until the match with the other camp was over.

Superordinate goals

This was the only approach that did reduce the conflict. In Carolyn Sherif's own words:

> Our final hypothesis was that the contact between equals, in order to cause change, had to involve interdependence of a kind that required the resources and energies of all the members of both groups. There had to be some goal to be achieved in the environment that they couldn't ignore, but that everyone was needed to do. We called those 'superordinate goals'[8]

It is important to emphasise that these goals had to be 'engineered' by the staff running the camp. For example, they sabotaged the water supply in such a way that it could not be mended unless both groups pitched in. Also it was only after a number of these goals had been introduced that the conflict subsided.

Explaining the conflict

Having established that groups can have great difficulty in communicating with one another on friendly terms, it remains to ask why this should be the case. Must competition inevitably lead to destructive and unnecessary conflict? The Sherifs' own explanation can be summarised as the following chain of events:

- realistic conflict of interests
  leads to:
- competition
  which leads to:
- strong identification with the in-group
  which leads to:
- discrimination against the out-group

Study 2: Tajfel and minimal groups

A different line of explanation was established by British and European researchers led by Henri Tajfel. Noting that there was some evidence of intergroup discrimination between Sherifs' groups even before the competitive activities had started, he designed a series of experiments to test the Sherifs' ideas, and to discover the minimal conditions for intergroup behaviour. Consider how you might have reacted as a subject in one of those early experiments:

You are a British schoolboy whose class has been volunteered to participate in a study on decision-making. The psychologists tell you that you are in group A and that the other members of your class are either in group A or group B. You do not know who is in which group and your classmates do not know which group you are in. You are then given a series of pencil and paper tasks which ask you to distribute sums of money to members of group A and group B. On each task you are given a range of possible choices which will mean different amounts of money going to other members of the group. For example suppose you had to choose between the three alternatives given in Table 23. In the actual experiment, you would have been confronted with many more alternatives but these examples do illustrate very different strategies: do you favour your own group (A); do you go for fair and equal distribution (B); or do you

Table 23

	Alternative A	Alternative B	Alternative C
To group A	7	13	19
To group B	1	13	25

extract as much money as possible from the experimenters while favouring members of the other group (C)?

Would it not be most logical to go for alternative C and extract the most money? Why should you discriminate between the groups on any basis – you do not know who is in which group and the assignment of groups was arbitrary.

Despite this seeming arbitrariness, the boys typically went for alternative A, favouring their 'own' group even at the expense of gaining more money. After repeating this experimental design on many occasions and finding the same general results, Tajfel concluded that this could be explained by a more fundamental process of social identification which led to discrimination and conflict. In contrast to Sherif, he proposed a chain of events as follows:

- social categorisation
  leads to:
- social identity
  which leads to:
- social comparison
  which leads to:
- psychological distinctiveness
  which leads to:
- self-esteem

In other words, you place yourself (or are placed) in a particular social category and this becomes part of your social identity. For this to be meaningful, you have to compare your group (category) with other categories. When you make this comparison, you look for something distinctive or positive. Thus, your group is seen as better than the group you have compared yourself with. This satisfies your motivation to be a person of some value, i.e. to have high self-esteem. The development of this perspective provided the basis for social identity theory which in turn inspired an upsurge of interest in intergroup problems.[9] This led to research which tested Tajfel's basic propositions. Generally these were supported, but not always. For example, discrimination between groups does not necessarily follow as a result of relevant social comparison as Tajfel would predict – group membership can mean very different things to different people in different situations.

The ideas presented in earlier chapters of this book on the distinction between personal and social identity are based on more recent developments of this theory – self-categorisation – the idea that, when we categorise ourselves as members of a group, we perceive ourselves in relation to our notion of the group prototype and judge our own and others' behaviour accordingly.[10]

We must also not forget broader factors – both Sherif and Tajfel would emphasise that psychological explanation must be seen alongside consideration of social and historical factors. For example, Sherif's summer camp groups were equally powerful. What would have happened if one group had been more powerful than the other? In many real-life situations, we are only too aware that the other group is more or less powerful than we are. And this takes us to consider a situation where power relationships are very clear-cut: the prison.

Study 3: Zimbardo's prison

Having become interested in issues of prisoner behaviour, Philip Zimbardo decided to observe the processes at first hand by setting up a simulated prison in the basement of his department building, which he tried to make as authentic as possible with official uniforms and procedures.[11] He recruited student volunteers at 15 dollars a day (still worth something back in 1973). They were told that the study was due to last two weeks and that they would be randomly assigned by a flip of a coin to be either prisoners or guards. He made sure that all the volunteers were screened to eliminate any subjects who had psychological or emotional problems.

The guards were issued with identical uniforms, including large sunglasses, a large club, whistle and cell keys. They were talked through the ground rules which were established for the experiment, the most significant being that the guards were expected to control the prisoners and implement rules and discipline but were not permitted to use any physical violence. Zimbardo had enlisted help from the local Palo Alto police so the prisoners were put through a 'real' arrest and booking procedure, including being handcuffed, fingerprinted, and stripped.

Before you read on, consider your initial reactions and expectations in this situation, remembering the following points:

• As a prisoner you have been surprised by the authenticity of the arrest and booking which happened unexpectedly. You have been stripped and given a long lecture on the rules of the prison. You have now been herded into a 6 foot by 9 foot cell with two other prisoners, all wearing this anonymous 'smock-like' uniform and stocking caps on their heads and addressed as a 'real' criminal. This is the first time you have been locked up in any sense – how do you feel? You have to ask the guards permission to do anything, even go to the toilet – is this experience worth 15 dollars a day?

• As a guard you are now kitted out in this standard uniform. You have met the other guards and have been given a detailed briefing on the rules of the place. You know that the study will only last a couple of weeks but you have been placed in this position of power and authority. How do you propose to exercise this authority? And how do you feel towards this group of prisoners who have just filed in?

In some ways, this study is reminiscent of the Milgram experiments – the study was set up with only very general expectations of what would emerge and the researchers very soon became astonished at the behaviour they observed. Zimbardo abandoned the experiment after only six days at a point where he was concerned that any further continuation could endanger the psychological health of the participants, especially the prisoners. After one brief attempt to 'revolt', the prisoners had become demoralised and depressed to such an extent that Zimbardo was forced to intervene. The guards rapidly engaged in cruel and repressive actions towards the prisoners which were totally out of proportion – demanding roll-calls in the middle of the night, withdrawing basic privileges more or less on a whim. In both groups, strong conformity pressures were evident: after the crushed revolt, any prisoner who showed any signs of independence was derided by the other prisoners as a 'trouble-maker'; any guards who seemed reluctant to participate in the prisoners' repression was given a hard time by the other guards.

Zimbardo had expected the groups to take on their respective roles but was horrified by the speed and intensity of the changes. He concluded that the participants had been deindividuated – the anonymity which had been forced on them had deprived them of their normal sense of responsible social behaviour and they had been completely 'taken over' by the perceived demands of the role. The main features of this process are summarised in Table 24. Perhaps it is not surprising that after the study Zimbardo went on to do considerable work arguing for prison reform.[12]

Table 24

Presence of group leads to	Intervening psychological change	Output
Anonymity	Loss of identity	Behaviour not under usual social/ personal controls
Diffused responsibility	Reduced concern for social evaluation	Impulsive irrational behaviour

Although a quarter of a century has passed since the Stanford Prison Simulation, we can still speculate on the most plausible explanation. For example, how do we explain what happened to the guard who wrote in his private diary before the study:

> As I am a pacifist and nonaggressive individual, I cannot foresee a time when I might maltreat other living things.[13]

By the fifth day of the study this same guard was writing:

> I harass Sarge who continues to stubbornly overrespond to commands. I have singled him out for special abuse both because he begs for it and because I simply don't like him.

Evaluating Zimbardo's explanation

Zimbardo's own explanation was in the power of the social situation over the individual and the process of deindividuation. Other commentators have also focused on the role demands involved.

Recently Stuart Carr has suggested that neither of these explanations is very convincing and that we need to look for the way that the role-players' perceptions of the other participants may have changed during the course of the experiment.[14] We know that individuals often rationalise any perceived inconsistencies between their own attitudes and their behaviour. In particular, Carr quotes the 'Principle of Minimal Sufficiency' where someone has complied to act in a particular way which is contrary to their general beliefs and where the pressure to comply has been gentle or mild. In this circumstance, you find it difficult to justify your compliance and so you are likely to change your attitudes in line with your behaviour.

There are examples from the history of brainwashing where relatively mild and consistent pressure has proven effective in changing prisoners' attitudes, presumably because of this principle.

How could this principle relate to Zimbardo's guards? They were given the job of controlling the prison around the clock. Carr suggests that the groundrules at the start of the experiment were not very tight or specific. The guards had to exert authority in this situation. As they knew they were chosen to be guards by chance, could this also have influenced their perception? As a guard, you have been asked to exert control and authority but you do not feel as though you have much justification for your actions. You have complied with the relatively mild pressure to participate, and you know you could just as easily have been a prisoner. How do you justify your actions? Carr uses these ideas from attribution theory to suggest the guards justified their actions and escaped from any feelings of guilt at the time by 'blaming the victims', in this case the prisoners.

But this explanation also begs a few questions. Why did the participants take the situation so seriously in the first place? They knew it was only a simulation with a limited time span.

Zimbardo has also used a variation of the Milgram experiment – learner subjects giving electric shocks to 'stooge' learners – where it was found that increasing or decreasing the anonymity of the learners affected their willingness to administer shocks. For example, when participants felt more anonymous – asked to wear a large shapeless smock and hood with eyeholes – they administered longer shocks than when their personal identity was emphasised by being in normal clothing and given large name tags.

However, although there are subsequent studies which support Zimbardo's conclusion, there are also studies which show that increasing anonymity within a group can reduce aggression. Reicher and others have offered an explanation for these findings by modifying Zimbardo's notion of deindividuation as we see later in this chapter.

Study 3: Reicher's crowd

In the spring of 1980, there was a disturbance in the city of Bristol, in a working-class area in the centre of the city with no real history of crowd unrest. Following a raid on a local cafe which was designed to investigate accusations of illegal drug-taking, the police involved were pelted with stones and forced to withdraw.

After the arrival of police reinforcements, the incident degenerated into much more serious violence: police cars and other vehicles were set on fire, some shops and business premises were damaged, forty-nine policemen were injured, and the neighbourhood became a 'no-go' area for police for much of the night. By the following morning, the disturbance was over.

By the standards of other British and American riots in the 1980s, this was not a very serious event. But it has received a very detailed analysis from Steve Reicher, a social psychologist who was living in Bristol at the time.[15] Contrary to the media representation of St Paul's as an uncontrolled riot, Reicher noted that the violence was aimed at very specific targets, notably the police. The fact that the violence was also contained within a very specific geographical area also suggests that this was not the random expression of an uncontrolled mob. In fact, the crowd involved was almost entirely drawn from the neighbourhood community: people who knew each other well and who felt strongly identified with and proud of their community.

Does this situation lend itself to an analysis in terms of deindividuation, along the lines of Zimbardo? Or do we have to go back to notions of the irrational 'group mind' which was a popular notion earlier in this century?[16] Reicher argues otherwise: rather than a 'loss' of identity in these circumstances, members of crowds and groups experience a change in identity. The consequence of this change is that group members take on the group norms of behaviour, which may be quite different to their personal standards.[17] In a situation like St Paul's where the group feels threatened and 'invaded', then the emerging norm is one of violence and counter-attack.

Important concepts

There are a number of important concepts we can use to make sense of this variety of studies:

Group membership and social identity

In all these studies we have seen group members developing strong senses of their group identities and how this has been supported by the processes of categorisation and stereotyping (both of others and of self). Group boundaries have become solid and communication across the boundaries is used to escalate the negative stereotyping and conflict.

Power and social control

The introduction of the power dimension is critical as we can see by comparing the outcomes of Sherif – where both groups became more cohesive – and Zimbardo – where the powerless group became demoralised and passive. There is also the fact that a third group, the researchers, were active in each situation and were able to intervene before events got completely out of hand.

The salience of situations

In Chapter 2 we introduced the idea of the interpersonal–intergroup continuum (Tajfel) whereby individuals classify situations in terms of whether they are interpersonal or group. There is a more elaborate version of this which is worth considering in this context, developed by Geoffrey Stephenson. He suggests that the continuum is not the best way of representing how people respond to situations. For example, in his own studies of bargaining and negotiation, he noticed that: 'Negotiators may be intensely responsive to both interpersonal and intergroup considerations at one and the same time.'[18] So it is possible that both the interpersonal and intergroup dimensions of a situation can vary at the same time. This can be represented as a diagram as in Figure 6.[19]

A lengthy face-to-face negotiation between representatives of groups (management/union perhaps) would occupy position A. A telephone negotiation would be more likely in position C. A conversation between two very close friends would be in position B and position D is the queue at a bus stop.

Practical implications and issues

The previous discussion has suggested that it is relatively 'easy' to introduce conflict in intergroup situations. You could also argue that a certain degree of conflict or tension might be inevitable if the group comparison processes suggested by social identity theory are active.

On a more optimistic note, we can sugggest that this research demonstrates the importance of negotiation and communication processes across group boundaries. The more that group representatives are aware of the likely dynamic and power relationships in the situation, the better they can act to reduce or eliminate unecessary conflict and focus on the real differences or issues between the groups. This leads to the following practical suggestions:

- Group members should be aware of typical intergroup phenomena so that they can be cautious in their assumptions and opinions regarding the other group. Asking the group members to summarise their views of 'us' and 'them' can be a useful exercise – you can often see good–bad mirror images being expressed and this can lead to a discussion of the evidence (or lack of it) on which these views are based. This sort of reflection can be a revealing exercise as it can deflect members from jumping to unwarranted conclusions and developing 'us–them' attitudes. In other words, members should try to avoid the typical perceptual biases.
- Group representatives should try to avoid win–lose situations and attempt to clarify their group's role and position in each and every negotiation with the other group.

Communication is obviously very important as it underpins both these points. For a comprehensive review of detailed research on

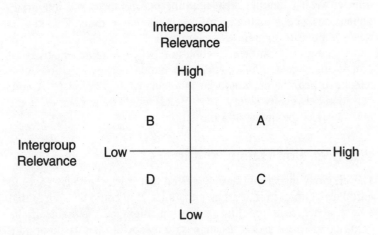

Figure 6

aspects of intergroup communication, see the recent book edited by Gudykunst[20] which also starts from ideas of social identity theory and Stephenson's bipolar diagram described above. Another practical suggestion which emerges from this volume is the notion that group representatives and members should be aware of the communication rules which are used by the other group. This can be especially important where there are cultural differences between the two groups. For example, Cushman and King analyse the difficulties which might be experienced due to different rules governing friendship formation in Japanese and American cultures.[21] Whereas Americans seem to follow a single type of friendship formation sequence so that the transition between acquaintance to good friend is a matter of increasing commitment, the Japanese draw a distinction between two types of friendship formation: interpersonal relationships which are developed out of social obligation; and close personal friendships. An American attempting to forge a friendship across this cultural boundary will have to decide how to relate to these different expectations.

One final, perhaps less optimistic, point is that the success of communication strategies will depend on whether members and leaders actually want to come to terms with one another, despite their differences. As we have seen from recent turmoil and warfare across the globe, in many situations the differences between groups are so emotionally charged that such willingness will not exist. Without this willingness, it is difficult to imagine strategies which will resolve the conflict, although this does not mean we should stop trying!

Notes

1 Although now some thirty years old, the book by Sherif is well worth reading: Sherif, M. (1969) *Social Psychology*. New York: Harper and Row.
2 For a recent discussion of the possible explanations of prejudice in social and psychological terms, see: Brown, R. (1996) *Prejudice. Its Social Psychology*. Oxford: Blackwell.
3 The Sherifs' own account of the summer camp experiments can be found in their 1961 book. A good secondhand account is in Chapter 15 of Raven and Rubin: Sherif, M., Harvey, O. J., White, B. J., William, R. and Sherif, C. W. (1961) *Intergroup Conflict and Cooperation: The Robbers Cave Experiment*. Norman, OK: University Book Exchange; Raven, B. H. and Rubin, J. Z. (1983) *Social Psychology*, 2nd edn. New York: John Wiley.

4 See the interview with Muzafer and Carolyn Sherif in: Evans, R. I. (1980) *The Making of Social Psychology: Discussions with creative contributors*. New York: John Wiley.

5 For examples of how this work can be applied, see the work of Blake and Mouton: Blake, R. and Mouton, J. (1962) The intergroup dynamics of win–lose conflict and problem-solving collaboration in union–management relations. In Sherif, M. (ed.) *Intergroup Relations and Leadership*. 94–140. New York: John Wiley.

6 From a theory developed by Newcomb: Newcomb, T. (1947) Autistic hostility and social reality. *Human Relations*, 1, 69–86.

7 See Raven and Rubin pages 651ff. (note 3).

8 See note 4.

9 For an overview of Tajfel's work and the development of social identity theory see Chapters 2 and 3 in Turner and Giles or either of Tajfel's own works: Tajfel, H. (ed.) (1978) *Differentiation between Social Groups: Studies in the social psychology of intergroup relations*. London: Academic Press; Tajfel, H. (ed.) (1982) *Social Identity and Intergroup Relations*. Cambridge: Cambridge University Press; Turner, J. C. and Giles, H. (eds) (1981) *Intergroup Behaviour*. Oxford: Basil Blackwell.

10 The development of social identity theory and ideas of self-categorisation are explained and discussed in: Turner, J., Hogg, M., Oakes, P., Reicher, S. and Wetherell, M. (1987) *Rediscovering the Social Group*. Oxford: Blackwell.

11 See Zimbardo's 1973 article for his own version of events. For a good secondhand account, see pages 558ff. of Raven and Rubin (note 3 above): Zimbardo, P. G., Haney, C., Banks, W. and Jaffe, D. (1973) A Pirandellian prison: The mind is a formidable jailer. *New York Times Magazine* 8 April, 38–60.

12 For a recent discussion of the impact and significance of this study, see the following article based on an interview with Zimbardo a few years ago: McDermott, M. (1993) On cruelty, ethics and experimentation. Profile of Philip G. Zimbardo. *The Psychologist*, October, 456–9.

13 These quotes are taken from the article by Stuart Carr: Carr, S. (1995) Demystifying the Stanford Prison study. *BPS Social Psychology Section Newsletter*, 33, 31–4.

14 See note 13.

15 Reicher provides a detailed analysis of the disturbance in: Reicher, S. (1984) The St Pauls Riot: An explanation of the limits of crowd action in terms of a social identity model. *European Journal of Social Psychology*, 14, 1–21.

16 The concept of the group mind was first popularised by Gustave Le Bon at the turn of the century. His textbook of the time has been reprinted. See Chapter 1 of Brown's work for a modern perspective on this work: Le Bon, G. (1908) *The Crowd: A study of the popular mind*. London: Unwin; Brown, R. (1988) *Group Processes*. London: Basil Blackwell.

17 To see how Reicher is now developing these ideas, see: Reicher, S. and Levine, M. (1994) Deindividuation, power relations between groups

and the expression of social identity: The effects of visibility to the out-group. *British Journal of Social Psychology*, 33, 145–63.

18 Stephenson's research on negotiation and bargaining is very relevant to the concerns of this chapter. For a brief summary, see his article which is Chapter 6 in Turner and Giles (note 9).

19 Based on the figure in the Stephenson article.

20 Especially see Gudykunst's own chapters (1 and 13) in: Gudykunst, W. B. (ed.) (1986) *Intergroup Communication*. London: Edward Arnold.

21 The article by Donald P. Cushman and Sarah Sanderson King is Chapter 4 of the book by Gudykunst, note 20.

Part III

Chapter 10

Getting groups to work – teams in organisations

Group and team development have become increasingly important over the last decade in all types of organisations, given some of the changes in our economic and political environment. And some research has focused on the characteristics of effective teams at different levels of the organisation. For example, Bantel and Finkelstein[1] have investigated the key attributes of top management teams and concluded that top team structures are dependent upon three sets of factors: environmental, strategic and organisational. Environmental factors include the levels of uncertainty and stability. Strategic factors include the level of diversification in the company. Organisational factors include its technology, size and age.

However, the focus of this chapter is more on new developments in teamworking strategies and team development. These have become very important themes in modern management literature. After briefly summarising important concerns which have persuaded business and commercial organisations to move towards a greater emphasis on teamwork, we then look at major aspects of this new emphasis: the debate over the characteristics of effective teams; work on the development of effective team structures within organisations; the types of team-building interventions which are being employed; and some implications of these developments for other areas in this book.

The final part of the chapter looks at some of the cautionary tales and reservations about the spread of team methods, and suggests some general implications.

Organisations in context and the move to teams

The increasing economic pressures on business and commerce have led a number of organisations to adopt radical strategies to remain competitive. The daily papers regularly present headlines of job cuts (or downsizing in management-speak) or major restructuring or usually both. The management literature of the 1990s is also full of new strategies which supporters claim will provide organisations with the desired upturn in their economic fortunes. A good example of one of these strategies and one of the recent buzz-words (or should it be buzz-phrases?) has been Business Process Re-engineering (BPR).

BPR consultants will recommend that the organisation must take a radical and fundamental look at what it does and how it does it. They will also advise the organisation that it must have the ambition to make a major improvement to its productivity and must have no qualms at discarding or breaking old rules. Concentrating on how things are done and how customers are treated becomes of paramount concern. There is also heavy emphasis on the creative use of information technology to increase efficiency. As a result, the organisation will tend to move away from department structures to using project teams, to providing workers with more skills and opportunities, and to focus on worker education rather than training. It is ironic that this movement has more recently been criticised for being too obsessed with cost-cutting and not paying sufficient attention to its impact on people.[2]

One common theme in these initiatives is an emphasis on teamworking, usually coupled with the suggestion that we need to move away from traditional hierarchical structures:

> Teams will be the primary building blocks of the organisation of the future.[3]

New team structures in organisations

One strand of work which is very relevant to the purposes of this book concerns recent attempts to define self-managing or self-directed teams (SDTs). You can find many enthusiastic advocates of SDTs – formal groups of multi-skilled employees who are given a range of responsibilities which previously would have been allocated to a manager, ranging from planning work schedules through to hiring new staff. For example, Richard Wellins describes SDTs as 'one of the most powerful empowerment strategies available to today's companies' which can prove to be 'an exciting innovation for the improvement of employees' workplace participation, productivity, and quality of life'.[4]

The amount of self-regulation allowed to these working teams varies between different organisations but the important common features include:[5]

- the responsibility for a complete job or operation within the workplace
- a significant degree of autonomy in decision-making
- a significant degree of control over their daily work behaviour

The implications for team leaders

One major implication of this move is that the role of team leader no longer exists in the same way. Some authors seem to take the view that leadership is no longer needed. Others see it as a change from traditional models of supervision to more of a coaching role, whereby the role is to help the members of the group work towards autonomy.[6] Hackman[7] argues that leadership becomes even more important in these groups than in traditional organisations.

Defining effective teams in organisations

Wellings defines the key factors of effective teams as: commitment; trust; purpose; communication; involvement; and process orientation (which he defines as having a range of tools such as problem-solving techniques which will help the group achieve its goals).[8]

A similar list comes from a leading team of management consultants.[9] They include clarity in team goals; clearly defined roles; clear communication; beneficial team behaviours (what we described earlier as positive task and social behaviours); well-defined decision procedures; balanced participation; established ground rules; and awareness of the group approach. They also add an improvement plan – including a flow chart of the project in hand which defines necessary resources and assistance – and use of the scientific approach – which is the insistence that opinions are supported by data and that the group avoids jumping to conclusions and unwarranted assumptions.

These characteristics will not come as any great surprise to anyone who has read through the previous chapters of this book and you will also find other very similar lists in other texts.[10] Michael West offers one way of clustering these characteristics in a way which also relates back to previous chapters.[11] He suggests three main components: the extent to which the team meets task objectives; the extent to which it maintains the team members' individual well-being; and the extent to which the group continues to work together. Using the two task and social elements, he defines four extreme types of group. The fully functioning team is high on all three components; the dysfunctional team is low on all. The cold efficiency team is high on task effectiveness but average/low on the other components; the cosy team is average/low on all.

What is not clear from these lists and category schemes is the causal relationship between the different characteristics. For example, early work on leadership styles often assumed that worker satisfaction would lead to productivity. This relationship did not always materialise. If we are not sure about the causal links then how do we decide to intervene and improve the situation? Is there one overriding factor which will then deliver the other desired consequences?

West places major emphasis on the team vision and considers that an effective vision must have the following characteristics. It must be clear so that everyone knows exactly what is involved. It must have motivating value so that everyone is engaged and committed. It must be attainable to keep everyone motivated. It must be shared and this will depend upon how it was developed. And finally it must be able to develop in order to reflect the changing environment and changes within the group. Those of you who work in large organisations with mission statements are invited to consult it now to see if it reflects a vision which has these characteristics. If it does not, then . . . .

An alternative emphasis comes from Katzenbach and Smith who define five transition stages in the move from working group to high-performing team:[12]

- the working group interact to share information and make decisions but do not have a realistic, shared overall purpose which calls for a team approach
- the pseudo-team is a group which could be a significant team but has no interest in shaping a common purpose and is not trying to do so
- the potential team is trying to improve its collective performance but is not yet clear enough about common goals or accountability

- the real team is committed to common goal(s) and feels account-able for their mutual working approach
- the high-performance team is a real team plus the real commit-ment of every member to each other's personal growth

Katzenbach and Smith consider that high-performance teams are rare in organisations and unfortunately I have to agree. Take a moment to reflect on your organisation – can you think of *one*?

The key characteristic of an organisation which will allow high-performance teams to develop is what they call its performance ethic. Unless clear and consistent performance standards are demanded of the group then it will not develop the commitment and concern to become high-performing. But it is not just a case of setting a difficult task. To quote the approach used by the staff of one leading British management college:

> One of the big mistakes of the past has been to work with the false assumptions that if a group of people are given a challen-ging and exciting enough job to do, success will follow.[13]

They advocate a vision of superteams which demonstrate qualities very similar to Katzenbach and Smith's high-performing teams. Once again the team is characterised by expectations and striving for outstanding performance. Strategies and skills required to create such teams include negotiating the success criteria, planning both the goals and the process, effective leadership, and dealing with the specific environment.

Contrast these recipes for success with the models expressed in many manuals of team development in organisations. For example, Mike Woodcock proposes four stages of team development.[14] At stage one, the team shows a number of fundamental weaknesses, including poor listening, unclear objectives and dependence on the boss to make most of the decisions. At stage two, members start to show more concern for each other, listening improves and there is some discussion of personal feelings. At stage three, this team spirit is maintained and more methodical work procedures are implemen-ted according to a clear and understood set of groundrules. At stage four, all these improvements are maintained and the team shows much more flexibility with development becoming a priority. This model effectively urges teams to work on their interpersonal and social processes as a prelude to developing more effective working methods. And this brings us to the range of team-building methods now in use.

Team-building methods and techniques

In the 1960s or 1970s, organisations were being urged by many external consultants to use methods of group training such as T Groups (which are discussed in Chapter 12) and which aim to uncover:

> information about feelings and interpersonal behaviour as an important element, information that is usually suppressed or overlooked in formal, hierarchically structured organisations.[15]

The assumption was that groups which could come to terms with their interpersonal underworld and processes would be able to work together much more closely and co-operatively. This assumption was challenged and these group methods were replaced by approaches which paid more attention to task concerns and which were not so firmly rooted in explicit values of openness and trust.

It is perhaps worth drawing a distinction between methods which are recommended as part of a more ambitious move towards team-based organisation and interventions which can be used by organisations which are not necessarily planning such a major cultural shift.

Teamwork as organisational design

A typical example of this approach is the work by Dean Tjosvold who talks of team work as offering a 'competitive advantage' to organisations which use it. Not surprisingly from this viewpoint, he starts by emphasising the importance of establishing the vision for the team which should 'portray an uplifting and ennobling future'.[16] Several characteristics of this vision are critical and he echoes the recommendations given by West above. He also emphasises the need to create this vision in a series of stages:

- setting the stage, where there must be open discussion and resolution of any long-standing conflict before starting work towards the new vision
- challenging the status quo, where there must be genuine debate about what needs to change

- team commitment, where the vision is reinforced by the open involvement of the team in discussion and debate
- ongoing review, to ensure that complacency does not set in

This concern for proper planning and open communication is also found in the later stages of the move to team work which focuses on creating unity in the team and empowering the team members.

Empowering is described by Tjosvold as the feeling that 'we can do it', based on group cohesion and confidence which is fully supported by the organisation.[17] This concept which occurs frequently in this literature is not uncontroversial: 'Perhaps no concept has garnered more attention or caused more contention than empowerment'.[18] One reason for the controversy is that empowerment can be defined at various levels. From a psychological point of view, you may feel empowered if your contribution to the team is recognised and valued, if you feel that what you do is important, if you feel some degree of control over what you do and how you do it, and if you feel that you can affect the way your team operates. But you can also define empowerment at an organisational level where individuals are empowered by an organisation which shares information, rewards, knowledge and power.[19] Although these definitions are related, they are also in potential conflict. The definition of empowerment adopted by many organisations is very limited and may not be sufficient to make any profound impact on individuals and groups.

Mending teamwork

West suggests that there are five main types of team-building interventions. These have different aims and scope and will satisfy different needs and different situations:[20]

Team start-up

A newly formed team may need work on clarifying the team objectives, deciding the member's roles and co-ordination, and other forming issues.

Regular formal reviews

This may involve 'away-days' where the team takes a day out of the usual routine and environment to reflect on how things are going and being done.

Addressing known task-related problems

This also involves some time out but perhaps not so much as an away-day to focus on a very specific problem.

Identifying problems

This is where the focus of the team review is on identifying task-related problems, where a team feels that it is not functioning as effectively as it could but is not sure why. This may involve discussion or some questionnaire analysis or use of an external facilitator.

Social process interventions

Here the focus is very much on the social climate and member relationships.

As with the more profound attempts to change organisation culture, all these interventions require skilled and careful implementation or they can be subverted to fuel existing conflicts and resentments. Intergroups are an important feature of organisation life and all the cautionary tales of Chapter 9 are relevant here. There are also other important variants of these strategies which we cannot cover in any depth here. For example, the use of outdoor activities as the focus for team-building is now well-established in the UK and has some very enthusiastic advocates.

But will teams win the day?

Needless to say, not everyone is convinced that the way forward for large organisations is to move to team-based structures. There are two main lines of opposition: one based upon the conviction that other forms of organisation are preferable, and the other which highlights the practical difficulties of implementing team-based structures.

Back to managerial leadership

One of the most eloquent opponents of this move to teams is Elliot Jaques who suggests that these ideas amount to 'a seriously disruptive movement' which is based upon 'unrealistic fantasies about what the managerial hierarchy should be'.[21] Although he is unhappy about many traditional managerial practices, he is even more unhappy about the possible lack of accountability in a team-based organisation. He is convinced that organisations must employ *individuals* who are accountable for the work of their subordinates, and that this accountability cannot be taken on by groups: 'individual managerial accountability does not, and cannot, disappear merely by the introduction of groupthink'.

Jaques' answer to struggling organisations is to adopt his ideas of managerial leadership by ensuring that there are not too many layers of management; by clarifying formal relationships across the organisation, by selecting effective individuals; by ensuring effective communication and dialogue between managers and subordinates; and by implementing fair pay and reward systems. For example, he suggests that many large organisations have up to twenty layers of management from shop floor to executive whereas not more than seven is necessary.

Groups are difficult, aren't they?

After reporting several examples where the adoption of teamworking has achieved major improvements in both productivity and worker satisfaction, Marchington quotes several studies which suggest that teamworking can have other less positive outcomes.[22] For example, it can create more pressure and stress, depending on the way that management set the team goals and targets. If the supervisory role is changed to one of facilitator or trouble-shooter, then the organisation needs people with the skills and confidence to take on this role. What happens to the former supervisors in this situation – will they have the skills and flexibility to adjust? This also raises broader questions of trade union involvement and co-operation.

This raises the point that we cannot simply expect the old hierarchical values and attitudes simply to melt away. Unless senior managers are committed to new ways of teamworking, they may well use their power and influence to dominate. Kanter describes four major 'inequalities' which will drive individuals away from full commitment to the team:[23]

The 'seductiveness of the hierarchy'

The team may well be assembled with members having very different statuses within the organisation. As individuals are aware of these differences, they may well behave according to them within the new team. The new co-operative team is actually controlled by the dominant members who simply reproduce the old hierarchy.

The knowledge gap

She also talks of the power of information where new members of the team may not have the necessary information to participate fully, or have the network of contacts to obtain it.

Different personal resources

Members come to the group with very different skills and resources. These differences can lead to counter-productive communication, for example, if sub-groups develop or if people do not have very strong skills in participation.

The seniority gap

More active or more senior members in the group itself may make newcomers less willing to speak up.

As a result of these inequalities, the participation in the team may be skewed towards those who already have formal power outside the group and team politics takes over as the driving force. A further problem is the suggestion that 'the idea of participation is imbued with a mystique that makes legitimate differentiation among participants difficult.' In other words, members cannot air legitimate differences because they feel that everyone has to act as if they were all equal. The 'myth' that this is a team becomes the dominant feeling inside the group and legitimate debate becomes stifled. Kanter's description of this process is rather like some of the processes we found in groups suffering from groupthink in Chapter 8.

And finally

This chapter has tried to illustrate the growing importance of team development in modern organisations. And there is no sign of enthusiasm waning as recent additions to the literature include further attempts to provide the definitive team-building handbook,[24] further advocates of the team as the building block of the organisation,[25] and further prescriptions for leadership with team-building skills.[26]

However, many current management texts do seem to underestimate how difficult it is to apply group and team concepts without falling into some of the traps and problems highlighted in earlier chapters of this book. The one thing we can be sure of is that these attempts to promote teams will become more rather than less important over the next decade – and the practice certainly will not get any easier.

Notes

1 Bantel and Finkelstein's article provides a useful summary of previous work on top management teams as well as a model of the important factors: Bantel, K. A. and Finkelstein, S. (1995) The determinants of top management teams. In Markovsky, B., Heimer, K. and O'Brien, J. (eds) *Advances in Group Processes*. 12, 139–65.

2 Hammer and Champy's book is one of the most readable introductions to this technique, and they also suggest ways in which organisations can make a mess of its introduction. Hammer, M. and Champy, J. (1995) *Re-engineering the Corporation*. Revised edn. London: Nicholas Brealey.

3 From page 173 of a very influential book on teams in organisations which I refer to several times in this chapter: Katzenbach, J. R. and Smith, D. K. (1993) *The Wisdom of Teams*. Cambridge, MA: Harvard Business School.

4 These quotes are from page 172 of the following book. Wellings's article describes what he calls the five major issues which must be dealt with to make self-directed teams work: Wellings, R. S. (1994) Building a self-directed work team. In Mabey, C. and Iles, P. (eds) *Managing Learning*, London: Routledge.

5 Mick Marchington provides some interesting examples in the 1994 extract from his 1992 book: Marchington, M. (ed.) (1992) *Managing the Team: A guide to successful employee involvement*. Oxford: Blackwell; Marchington, M. (1994) Job redesign. In Mabey, C. and Iles, P. (eds) *Managing Learning*, London: Routledge.

6 See: Manz, C. C. (1993) *Business Without Bosses*. New York: Wiley.

7 Hackman's book is relevant to several issues discussed in this book: Hackman, J. R. (ed.) (1990) *Groups That Work (and those that don't): Creating conditions for effective teamwork*. San Francisco: Jossey-Bass.

8 See note 4.

9 For a comprehensive overview of team development from a management consultancy perspective, see: Scholtes, P. R. *et al.* (1988) *The Team Handbook: How to use teams to improve quality*. Madison, WI: Joiner Associates.

10 For another business-oriented example, see: McWhirter, D. (1995) *Managing People: Creating the team-based organisation.* Holbrook, MA: Adams

11 For a very readable and comprehensive British introduction to this area, see: West, M. (1994) *Effective Teamwork.* Leicester: BPS Books.

12 See note 3.

13 The approach of Ashridge Management College is explained along with a range of case studies and examples in: Hastings, C., Bixby, P and Chaudry-Lawton, R. (1986) *Superteams: A blueprint for organisational success.* Glasgow: Fontana/Collins.

14 Woodcock bases his model on a list of criteria for effective teams, in: Woodcock, M. (1979) *Team Development Manual.* London: Gower.

15 See Chapter 6 of this book for a brief review of important organisational change strategies. The quote is from page 96: Blackler, F. and Shimmin, S. (1984) *Applying Psychology in Organisations.* London: Methuen.

16 Tjosvold has also published recent work on leadership which is relevant to the interests of this book. For the quote and discussion, see pages 124ff. of: Tjosvold, D. (1991) *Team Organization: An enduring competitive advantage.* Chichester: John Wiley.

17 See pages 150ff. of Tjosvold (note 16).

18 As discussed on page 255ff. of: Quinn, R. E., Faerman, S. R., Thompson, M. P. and McGrath, M. R. (1996) *Becoming a Master Manager: A competency framework,* 2nd edn. New York: John Wiley.

19 For discussion of empowerment from the organisational view, see: Bowen, D. E. and Lawler, E. E. (1991) The empowerment of service workers: What, why, how, where and when. *Sloan Management Review,* Spring, 31–9.

20 See the chapter in West (note 11).

21 The quotes are taken from page 182 of the article in Mabey and Iles (1994). Detailed explanation of Jaques's views can be found in the 1991 book: Jaques, E. and Clement (1991) *Executive Leadership.* Arlington, VA: Cason Hall & Co; Jaques, E. (1994) Managerial leadership: The key to good organization. In Mabey, C. and Iles, P. (eds) *Managing Learning,* London: Routledge.

22 See note 5.

23 For a brief summary of Kanter's views see the extract in Mabey and Iles: Moss Kanter, R. (1982) *The Change Masters: Corporate entrepreneurs at work.* London: Allen and Unwin; Moss Kanter, R. (1994) Dilemmas of teamwork. In Mabey, C. and Iles, P. (eds) *Managing Learning,* London: Routledge.

24 For example, see: Eales-White, R. (1995) *Building your Team.* London: Kogan Page.

25 For example, see: Phillips, N. (1995) *From Vision to Beyond Teamwork.* Chicago: Irwin.

26 For example, see: Katzenbach, J. and the RCL Team (1996) *Real Change Leaders.* London: Nicholas Brealey.

Chapter 11

Groups can help us learn – teamwork and students

This chapter provides a brief introduction to some important applications and implications of group and team dynamics in further and higher education. Are there changes afoot or can we still accept the following quote from a lecturer?:

> We all use it, but still we hardly ever teach it – groupwork in education.[1]

My own experience suggests that this is generally still true. Although students may spend a significant part of their time within a course working with other students, there is often very little attention paid to the skills necessary to support this interaction. But the picture is changing. In the same way that environmental change has persuaded many commercial organisations to invest in team development, many educational institutions are now placing more emphasis on students working in teams. These contextual changes are summarised in the first part of this chapter.

Not only are educational institutions placing more emphasis on students working in teams but those students are also being required to learn about the underlying group processes as they experience them. The variety of student life in groups is briefly summarised before examining these moves to group teaching and some typical recent initiatives. This leads into examples of student group interaction and the problems of staff intervention. The chapter finally raises some general issues for educational institutions who wish to make the most of student groups.

The changing educational context

A number of external factors have changed the face of higher education (HE) in the UK over the last couple of decades. For example, Brown and Knight highlight two key pressures: the expansion in HE and the increased pressures from the various 'stakeholders' (including funding bodies, students and employers) who are demanding that HE should become more accountable.[2] Brown and Knight see innovation and reform in assessment practices as the answer to these pressures.

These changes and pressures are echoed in other parts of the world. For example, a recent UNESCO report noted three key developments: major expansion in student numbers; major differentiation of institutional structures and forms/programmes; and financial restrictions.[3] These forces will continue to exert major pressures for change for the forseeable future. There have also been important political undercurrents to the changes and they have attracted critical comment which we should not ignore.[4]

Another major change which is important for this book is the dramatic upsurge of interest and research in learning and teaching methods – what has been called the 'scholarship of teaching'.[5] This leads to the confident assertion that:

> It is possible to change students' approach and the quality of their learning outcomes by manipulating those features of the context which the research has identified as crucial and especially by changing the assessment system.[6]

One feature that has received attention in this research is the quality of students' interaction with each other and there is now a growing literature on student groups which we return to later.[7] Another typical concern is the nature of the interaction between students and staff and the changing role-demands on staff when they move away from more conventional 'transmission' models of the teacher.[8]

Groups and student life

One problem with analysing the nature of group communication in any organisation is the variety of groups which it may be important to analyse. This is equally true of student life:

- Students often identify with their course or department, but this identification may be quite weak in comparison with other social identifications which students use.
- Students are organised into seminar groups, often on an arbitrary basis by alphabetical listing. Although these groups are an

important part of the quality of student experience, they may not meet very often during the week and have no life outside the scheduled contacts with staff.

- Sub-groups within the course group may be numerous and varied. For example, there may be sub-groups of mature students (e.g. married and/or older students, former Access students etc.), various friendship and/or flatmate groups, sub-groups of students from different ethnic backgrounds and so on. If you are on a course you may like to try a social analysis and identify the relevant sub-groups, and how their interaction affects the overall course experience.
- Sub-groups may develop in relation to the students' life outside college. We often run icebreaker workshops on new courses where we put students into groups selected at random and ask them to find out what they have in common. We imply that we select the groups on some non-random basis. This is an invitation to talk and share experiences which can very usefully break down some initial barriers. On one occasion, one of our random groups discovered they all shared a passion for motor bikes and they became a solid group for the rest of the course.
- Sub-groups within seminars or workshops may have a critical influence. Most college or university tutors will be able to remember one seminar group which gave them sleepless nights, where keeping the discussion going felt like pulling teeth without anaesthetic.

Rather than try to comment on all these permutations, the rest of this chapter will focus on the dynamics of the seminar and project groups.

However, there is one important implication of this variety, an implication which is also important in the consideration of any groups within large organisations. We cannot take it for granted that individual students will share the same feelings of loyalty and commitment to the course or seminar or project group.

There are two further complications to consider in the dynamics of student groups which are not the same in other types of organisations:

- the role of staff, especially in their duties as assessors
- the potential conflict between group and individual work in the relentless pursuit of better grades

We shall return to these issues after looking at some examples of récent initiatives in group teaching.

The rise of group teaching

Students now spend more time in project or small group discussions, partly as a response to the economic pressures mentioned above – rising numbers of students and falling numbers of staff – and partly for sound educational reasons – including responding to the continuing claims by employers that graduates lack sufficient communication and team skills.[9] The incorporation of work on personal and social skills into the college and university curriculum has also been encouraged in the UK by awarding bodies, such as BTEC who have built core skills requirements into their qualifications, by government-financed initiatives such as Enterprise in Higher Education, which aimed to encourage universities to foster graduates' entreprenurial and leadership skills, and by other educational pressure groups such as Education for Capability.[10]

Trying to help the dynamics

The result of these pressures and initiatives is that methods to develop group and team skills have become much more common in college and university courses. For over twenty years we have been incorporating group exercises and activities on the communication courses we offer across this university.[11] During these years and especially in the last decade, many other areas have also adopted similar techniques and approaches. For examples, see the case studies summarised by David Jaques.[12] This expansion has also resulted in a broader range of materials which staff can use to support their teaching and student learning, such as the Skillpacks which have now been used by literally thousands of students here at Sheffield Hallam.[13] A few recent examples from this and other institutions will illustrate typical approaches:

In housing

Parsons and Drew[14] describe and evaluate a second year undergraduate module which was based on two design exercises which were done individually by students in previous years.

Students and other staff were consulted in advance to identify issues to be resolved. These issues included concerns about how this would impact on their individual grades, concerns about unequal contributions from group members, and concerns about how the groups would be formed. Models of groupwork issues from Tom Douglas[15] and self-managed learning from Ian Cunningham[16] were employed to develop the unit structures and procedures. Materials available to students included the Belbin Team Role inventory (see Chapter 7).

The most important features of the unit design which emerged from the evaluation were the importance of the assessment rules, the construction of the task, the organisation and logistics and the tutor support. The assessment was the most critical factor.

In engineering

Marshall and Roberts[17] describe the range of courses and materials they have incorporated into their business management teaching for engineering students, including:

- a two-day course on Action Centred Leadership.
- a twelve-week team project where students work in groups of eight to develop a business plan for a new product or service which could generate £1 million in its first year of trading. The plan has to be presented to professional standards. The group work is supported by a lecture and tutorial programme including topics from marketing, accountancy etc. There is also a 'consultancy' service where representatives from the groups have rationed access to professional advisors such as a local bank manager.
- a four-day course on team skills which includes a range of team exercises and techniques (including brainstorming) and which focuses upon crisis management.

They comment on the success of these initiatives but also note that they require increased levels of staff commitment.

In business

Plymouth Business School use group work projects along with a peer group support system as part of a first year undergraduate module which aims to develop effective group work skills.[18] There is also an induction programme which incorporates planned group work experiences supported by lectures, a self-learning manual and other theoretical input. This is all part of a staged approach designed to equip undergraduates with the skills needed during their industrial placement and in their later careers.

In social science

Mark Griffiths at Nottingham Trent University has experimented with several new teaching methods with his psychology students, including the use of small groups. He notes the the important point that preparation is a critical ingredient in the success of tutorless small groups. Not only must tutors understand their role in structuring and organising the group working, but students themselves must be carefully prepared in both the content and the process of group working.[19] Given such preparation then students can find group methods both more enjoyable and more productive than more traditional methods. Griffiths has demonstrated this, using a learning grid to replace lectures alongside groupwork.[20]

Going back to school

Another important example of how groupwork can be applied comes from Rowland.[21] This does involve first year sixth formers at school so strictly speaking it is outside the scope of this chapter. But it deserves a mention because of the way it used a commercial training organisation and applied models straight out of Chapter 10!

Members of the Coverdale Organisation organised an outdoor team programme for the children which incorporated the main features of their organisational training programme:[22]

- an overall task which was organised in steps as a 'storyline' so that each chapter could be reviewed
- regular process review on the group interaction
- emphasis on a systematic approach to team working which focuses on the setting of precise aims, handling information, breaking work up into chunks, planning and reviewing

The success of this and other similar programmes provides further encouragement to those who are extending this type of work through education.

Reviewing the initiatives

These necessarily superficial descriptions of these initiatives make them sound very straightforward and easy to implement. But anyone who has tutored in further or higher education for any length of time knows that the dynamics of the student group can involve very difficult issues. Can we be optimistic that the development of group skills in students will be increasingly successful?

On the one hand, we do now have a growing range of materials which have been developed specifically to use with students. As well as those mentioned in the previous section, we now have a range from student guides[23] through to activity packs[24] through to complete team-building programmes of the sort introduced in Chapter 10.[25]

On the other hand, we cannot guarantee that all teaching staff will have either the interest, enthusiasm or skills to implement these methods into the curriculum. There is also the difficulty which we hinted at in the previous section – staff have a variety of roles in relation to students and some of these may conflict. The project group which is struggling with interpersonal tensions may not wish to divulge their problems to the staff tutor who would like to help but who will also mark the project at the end of the term. Some of thse tensions are illustrated in the next section which looks at issues of intervention.

Tensions, conflicts, and intervention

In a team-building intervention in a commercial organisation, there is hopefully a clear understanding of the roles involved, either because an external consultant is involved or because the existing hierarchy is well understood. What happens when lecturing staff who do not have team-building as their recognised expertise try to work with student groups? Consider the following examples from my experience, put yourself in the lecturer role, and consider how you would intervene:

The intergroup

I remember vividly one seminar group from some years ago which could have self-destructed for reasons of intergroup conflict. There were five or six mature students in the seminar and they had decided to form a study group outside class to provide mutual support. Initially this seemed to have a demoralising effect on the other students, who were all recent school-leavers. After a few meetings the atmosphere in the group became tense and competitive. The younger students started to make contributions but many of these seemed to be directed at the mature students rather than helping the discussion. As tutor, I felt drawn into the role of referee.

Consider what you would have done as tutor before you read on.

Before the next class session I made sure I had a few casual conversations with seminar members and diagnosed a 'classic' intergroup conflict. The mature students felt threatened by the young students whom they saw as much more confident with the demands of university life such as examinations; the young students felt threatened by the mature students whom they saw as much more confident with the demands of university life such as speaking up in seminars and planning assignments and as demonstrated by their regular study group meetings. Notice the selective and 'mirror' perceptions here which have echoes of the Sherif summer camp in Chapter 9.

I did manage to get the whole group to discuss their differences in the next class meeting but this was very difficult. I sensed that both sub-groups felt that admitting the problem in public would lead to 'loss of face'. The atmosphere did improve but the sub-group boundaries never completely faded into the backgound.

The dominant democratic leader

The group of five business students had completed the problem-solving exercise and had achieved a good score. This was the 'warm-up' exercise before a much longer management game exercise which started the following week. We wanted the groups to reflect on their operations and develop some ground-rules to help them through the weeks to come. Wandering round the groups, we noticed that Alice had taken on the leadership of this group and was ordering the others to take on the tasks necessary to solve the problem. All communication was channelled through her. She managed this well but then it was a relatively simple problem. We reckoned that Alice would have to behave much more democratically to survive the pressures of the management game and we hoped that members of the group would raise that as an issue in the discussion. None of them did. Just the opposite happened as all the members enthused about what an open and democratic group it had been, a conclusion which none of the tutors could share.

Consider what you would have done as tutor before you read on.

In the general discussion, I made a few indirect comments about groups needing to monitor how they were organising themselves on an ongoing basis. We did not make any direct comments on this group's leadership style on the grounds that this would have been no use. The students would have seen this as an attack on their judgements and closed ranks against us. We would have created a very clear intergroup situation. The group did run into trouble in the management game and we did intervene at that point.

The nearly consensus

To be successful in the problem-solving exercise, the group had to achieve a consensus within a strict time limit. Conversation was becoming heated. As I walked over to announce that time was up, Bob leapt to his feet and asked for more time. I said this was not possible and asked if they had achieved consensus. In response, Bob waved his fists in the air, shouted at me, and pointed accusingly at Helen, 'But we do all agree – it's only her that won't see sense!'

Consider what you would have done as tutor before you read on.

We did try to get the group to talk about why they (and Bob in particular) were getting so heated about the exercise. But nobody listened as they were too busy mentally revisiting the conflict which had arisen. We did not repeat that exercise as we were not satisfied that the learning justified the pain and stress.

So how should we work with student groups and teams?

These examples emphasise that resolving student group differences and problems can be both difficult and time-consuming. It also needs committed staff who have had some training or development to equip them to confront the various levels of problems which are covered in this book. At a time of shrinking resources, such development and training may be thinly spread.

On a more general note, there are several issues which are raised by the examples and issues given above which any teamwork with students must resolve, either explicitly or implicitly:

What is the underlying model of the effective team?

Do we follow the logic of Katzenbach and Smith (Chapter 10) and decide that the performance ethic is the critical and crucial variable? Does that then dictate our role as tutors? Or are we more focused on the social and interpersonal dynamics?

Which strategy to use?

There are various team-building strategies available – which ones are most appropriate? In particular, when and how is it appropriate to work on the social process areas?

What do students need to know?

One major issue is the nature of the support and tuition given to students. If we provide students with theoretical input on group processes, how should this be delivered and how can it be integrated within the practical work? For example, if they come across a text extolling the virtues of brainstorming, should we be reminding them of the critical issues introduced in Chapter 1 of this book?[26]

Will students respond?

At the end of the day, we give students awards on an individual basis. Whereas an organisation can offer group bonuses and reward systems, this can only function to a limited extent in education. How do we deal with students who withdraw or refuse to participate to try to 'protect' their individual grades.

What is the role of staff?

Many of these initiatives talk of the changing role of staff – from tutor to facilitator – but what level of intervention can staff legitimately provide? This is directly analogous to the debate in organisations around the leader of SDTs and the suggestions that the role is really one of coaching. One difference here is that the 'coach' is also the 'assessor' and this dichotomy may be uncomfortable.

What should staff diagnose as potential group problems, and how?

For example, how far do we expect staff to take on the role of group coach? And do we expect their interventions to be based on explicit group theory? And at what level of group theory? For example, Wyn Bramley's guide to the tutor running groups is based on concepts from Bion and Foulkes, as we discussed in Chapter 3.[27]

Should staff social engineer?

For example, should we be creating seminar groups on the basis of a Belbin profile or some other model of effective co-operation. Or should we mimic the chaos of real life and rely on the pin in the name list as our random selector?

Notes

1 Quote from page 217 of: Silverlock, T. and Silverlock, M. (1995) Teachers, learning, ego and groups. *Groupwork*, 8.
2 See in: Brown, S. and Knight, P. (1994) *Assessing Learners in Higher Education*. London: Kogan Page.
3 The UNESCO report and other influential papers are summarised in: Tunnermann, C. (1996) A new vision of higher education. *Higher Education Policy*, 9, 11–27.
4 For example, see: Hartley, D. (1995) The McDonaldisation of Higher Education: Food for thought. *Oxford Review of Education*, 21, 409–23.
5 For example see the range of research reported in: Gibbs, G. (ed.) (1994) *Improving Student Learning: Theory and practice*. Oxford: Oxford Centre for Staff Development.
6 From the preface to Gibbs' book, note 5.
7 For a useful example of the growing literature on student groups, see: Thorley, L. and Gregory, R. (1994) *Using Group Based Learning in Higher Education*. London: Kogan Page.
8 One of the most powerful (and readable) recent texts which argues that we abandon 'transmission' models of education is: Sotto, E. (1994) *When Teaching Becomes Learning: A theory and practice of teaching*. London: Cassell.
9 For an interesting discussion of the purely educational reasons for using groups, see Chapter 1 of: Reynolds, M. (1994) *Groupwork in Education and Training: Ideas in practice*. London: Kogan Page.
10 For an introduction to the Education for Capability approach, see the

manifesto and opinion columns on pages 2–4 of the 1996 journal *Capability*, 2.

11 The manual which contains many of the exercises and approaches we used with students from a very wide range of disciplines was published as: Marshall, S. and Williams, N. (1986) *Exercises in Teaching Communication*. London: Kogan Page.

12 See Chapter 8 of perhaps the leading British text in this area: Jaques, D. (1991) *Learning in Groups*. 2nd edn. London: Kogan Page.

13 Our Skillpacks have now been published commercially with both staff and student manuals, covering a wide range of student skills including groupwork: Drew, S. and Bingham, R. (1996) *The Student Skills Guide*. London: Gower; Drew, S. and Bingham, R. (1996) *The Student Skills Tutor's Handbook*. London: Gower.

14 Parsons and Drew published this study in: Parsons, D. E. and Drew, S. (1996) Designing group project work to enhance learning: Key elements. *Teaching in Higher Education*, 1, 65–80.

15 The work of Tom Douglas has also cropped up on several occasions in this book. The book that Parson and Drew used was: Douglas, T. (1991) *A Handbook of Common Groupwork Problems*. London: Tavistock, Routledge.

16 See his work on learning sets: Cunningham, I. (1986) Self managed learning. In Mumford, A. (ed.) *A Handbook of Management Development*, 145–63. Aldershot: Gower.

17 Marshall and Roberts describe their approach and discuss some of the problems in the following articles: Marshall, P. and Roberts, A. (1995) Team Building 1. *The New Academic*, 4; Marshall, P. and Roberts, A. (1996) Team Building 2. *The New Academic*, 5, 1, 16–18.

18 This summary is based on the following two conference papers by staff from the Plymouth Business School at Plymouth University: Garland, D. Y. (1995) Preparing undergraduates for team working: A developmental approach. Paper presented to the Annual Conference of the Occupational Division and Section, University of Warwick; Garland, N. (1995) Effective group work in higher education: Issues and problems. Paper presented to the Annual Conference of the Occupational Division and Section, University of Warwick.

19 For further discussion of this issue and other material relevant to this chapter, see: Griffiths, S. and Partington, P. (1992) Enabling active learning in small groups. In *Effective Learning and Teaching in Higher Education*, Module 5, parts 1 & 2. Sheffield: CVCP.

20 The learning grid method is described and evaluated in the following article: Griffiths, M. (1996) The use of a learning grid in small group teaching. *Psychology Teaching Review*, 5, 25–34.

21 See in: Rowland, D. (1995) An outdoor teamwork programme for a group of first year sixth formers. *Groupwork*, 8.

22 This approach is described in; Taylor, M. (1992) *Coverdale on Management*. 2nd edn. Oxford: Butterworth Heinemann.

23 For a recent example, see: Rice, J., Saunders, C., O'Sullivan, T. and Rogerson, S. (1996) *Successful Group Work: A practical guide for students in further and higher education*. London: Kogan Page.

24 For a recent example which complements note 23, see the following pack which contains activities, case studies and examples: Rice, J., Saunders, C., O'Sullivan, T. and Rogerson, S. (1996) *Group Work*. London: Kogan Page.

25 There is also an instructor's manual to go with this student guide: Mears, P. and Voehl, F. (1995) *Team Building: A structured learning approach*. London: Kogan Page.

26 For example, see pages 109–11 of Jaques (note 12).

27 See: Bramley, W. (1979) *Group Tutoring: Concepts and case studies*. London: Kogan Page.

Chapter 12

Groups can help – groupwork and some final thoughts

The main aim of this chapter is to introduce and briefly review the development, varieties and outcomes of 'groupwork', where groups assemble not to carry out some activity or task but to focus on the members' own personal development or interactive skills. Along the way we shall introduce some techniques and look at practical applications and implications.

After explaining some of the major initiatives which contributed to the explosion of interest in groupwork in the 1960s and 1970s, this chapter shows how some of these initiatives have developed and been absorbed into other areas and how we can relate some of these ideas to current developments in self-help and support groups.

Finally this chapter reflects in general on the areas covered in this book and concludes that, although we now have significant under-standing of group interaction and communication, we must still be wary of over-generalising. There are still many important puzzles left to solve.

An introduction to 'groupwork'

Many of the previous chapters in this book have focused on the *study* of 'group dynamics' which involves the search for empirical general-isations, the use of experimental studies, and the application of theory. The notion of groupwork adopts a very different perspective, perhaps best summarised in the following quote:

> Group-work is a finite activity whereby a small group seek to create change within their own behaviour and feelings.[1]

For the purposes of this book, I am not including the various types of therapeutic groups although techniques which were originally pioneered in psychotherapy have since been adopted by groupwork practitioners. Of course, many of the insights and ideas covered in this book are relevant to therapy groups as you will find if you look at recent texts on their use. For example, one recent text by Barbara Posthuma contains discussion of group development using Tuckman's model, analysis of group roles and leadership styles and so on.[2] I am also neglecting formal social work groups for reasons of space although much of the material written on these groups also has wider currency.[3]

What this definition does mean is that we are adopting an experiential rather than an experimental approach where the key focus is on participants' perceptions and interpretations of what is happening in the group. As a result, the focus is on individual/group change, and not empirical generalisations.

Some early origins of groupwork

Although the development of experiential groups is a relatively recent phenomenon, some of the important ideas have quite a long history. The most important innovations were the development of sensitivity training throughout the 1950s and the explosion of the encounter group movement in the 1960s and 1970s. These are described below after briefly mentioning other early influences.

Psychodrama

In the early years of this century, Jacob Moreno noted that he could help patients deal with emotional problems by helping them to participate in role-plays which re-enacted the issues they were confronting.[4] He concluded that change arises through the portrayal of problems or issues and developed the principles of psychodrama. Many modern ideas of role-playing are based upon his early insights.

Psychoanalytic group work

We have already met the post-Second World War work of Wilfred Bion at the Tavistock Institute in Chapter 3. Two important ideas emerged from this work which played a part in the later development of groupwork: concepts of people living and supporting each other in the so-called therapeutic community, and the Tavistock

'Study Group' a particular variety of self-study group where the trainer takes on a 'consultant' role where he/she reflects and observes the group process while remaining detached/remote. In keeping with Bion's theories of different types of group, this is designed to surface the anxiety feelings of individuals in the group and allows members to explore their fantasies about authority.[5]

Sensitivity training and the emergence of the T Group

As with many other important ideas in social research the idea of sensitivity training emerged from some work undertaken by Kurt Lewin. He was responsible for devising a training programme known as the 1946 Human Relations Workshop which used a mix of lectures, discussion and role-play activities designed to help the participants improve their understanding and competence in group interaction. Every evening on the course the trainers gathered for an analysis of the day's work. Following a request from some of the participants, the course members were allowed to sit in on these staff discussions in the evening. What emerged was a lively debate on the group dynamics which had emerged during the day with staff and students offering very different perceptions of events. At the end of the course it was generally agreed that these after-hours discussions had been the most valuable part of the experience, allowing participants to see some of the diverse ways in which behaviours could be interpreted.

This experience prompted Lewin and his co-workers to devise a training method which captured the flavour of these discussions and allowed participants to reflect more actively on the meaning of their and others' behaviour in the group. This developed the idea of the 'training group' which became known universally as the T Group.[6]

The T Group

The main agenda for a T Group is a discussion of 'here and now' behaviour in the group. In other words, the emphasis is on the mutual sharing of perceptions about what is happening in the group at the moment. Members are encouraged to disclose their feelings and receive feedback. This notion of feedback where participants receive comments on their behaviour is critical to the success of the T Group and the characteristics of effective feedback are discussed below. The role of the group leader is to participate and offer observations which help to keep the group members focused on these issues and generally act as facilitator.

It is actually very difficult to describe the sensation and processes of a T Group on paper as it is so very different to conventional groups where there is usually some external agenda and where the present behaviour is rarely the explicit focus of attention. For example, there is usually a very awkward phase at the beginning where Tuckman's observations on 'forming' become very real – the members of the group are uncertain about what is going on and the trainer does not seem to be offering too much in the way of direction or structure. Sometimes one or more members express anger and frustration at the trainer who is not 'earning his/her corn'. This expression of resentment often acts as the catalyst which stimulates participation and more productive discussion of the group functions and processes.[7]

Useful feedback

The importance of feedback in the T Group process was soon recognised and this led to work on identifying the main characteristics of 'good' feedback.[8] Feedback should not be confused with criticism as the explicit aim of feedback is to provide the receiver with information which they can use to decide whether they need or wish to change their behaviour in order to improve their performance. Criticism can of course also fulfil this function but is often expressed in a hostile or ambiguous way which does not indicate a clear way forward to the receiver. Among the characteristics identified as components of good feedback were:

- Good timing: the feedback should be as close as possible to the behaviour in question.
- Accurate description: the feedback should clearly describe or specify the behaviour in question.
- Reactions without judgement: the feedback should reveal the sender's emotional reaction to the behaviour without making moral or ethical judgements about it.
- Agreement: the feedback should be endorsed by several people and not just be one person's reaction.

From T Group to institution

The early trials with T Groups were judged to be so successful that an organisation was founded to promote and research the method –

National Training Laboratories (NTL). T Groups also became a major technique used by trainers in organisations who were working on organisation change, using an approach which became known as Organisation Development (OD).[9]

The Encounter Group

Whereas the T Group was identified as a method primarily focused upon group skills, the next major innovation in groupwork technique came from trainers who wished to encourage what became known as personal learning or personal growth. A wide variety of techniques emerged under this banner, many using nonverbal techniques (such as the work of Bill Schutz at the Esalen Institute in California) and many liberally borrowing techniques from therapeutic work.[10]

Probably the best way of understanding the main elements of this approach is to focus on the work of one of its founding fathers – Carl Rogers.

Carl Rogers and Basic Encounter

Originally, Carl Rogers was a psychotherapist who worked with individual patients or clients. He developed very pronounced views on how a therapist should behave in a one-to-one situation which included the following recommendations and which had a profound effect on the development of counselling:

- Unconditional positive regard: the therapist should display warmth and caring for the client (positive regard) and this should not be dependent on the client behaving in a particular way.
- Acting as a model: the therapist should act in a way which the client can use as an example to copy. The therapist should be perfectly open and honest and be quite prepared to discuss his/her own feelings.
- 'Do not give advice': the role of the therapist is to help clients work through their own problems and arrive at their own solutions.

One way of interpreting these recommendations is to say that Rogers has provided a specific set of communication rules for therapists. He also hopes that members of the groups will adopt the same rules by following the leader's example.

Rogers started working with therapeutic groups almost by

accident. He soon became very enthusiastic about the advantage of working with groups rather than individuals after he 'experienced the potency of the changes in attitudes and behaviour which could be achieved in a group'. In practical terms he suggests that groups can have powerful and positive effects by enabling the following chain of events:

- members feel psychologically safe and free to express themselves
- members can express their immediate feelings to one another
- mutual trust develops
- members feel more confident and accepting
- members feel less inhibited and can try out new behaviour
- members can learn from one another

Thus, the norms of the group incorporate trust, acceptance, and innovation. When you feel you can trust others, and that they accept and value your personality then you will not be wary of trying out new behaviour and learning from others. In other words, your communication will become more 'open' – you will feel less restricted or embarrassed in discussing personal problems or anxieties. You will develop skills in self-disclosure.

Rogers felt so strongly about the 'liberating' effect of therapeutic group experience that he converted the methods into what he called the basic encounter group.[11] This is designed *not* as a therapeutic experience but as a way of enabling 'normal' people to gain insight into their own behaviour. The role of the leader and the overall process is much the same as described above. Again, Rogers is enthusiastic about the likely outcomes, claiming that this experience will make a major contribution to the participants' self-knowledge. The claim then is that in this type of group, individuals can come to recognise aspects of themselves and others in a much more fundamental way than is possible in the usual social or working relationships. The intended consequences of this increased self-knowledge is that individuals will be able to relate better to others, both in the group and later in everyday life situations.

Impact and effects

There is evidence to suggest that encounter groups can provide these results although they are perhaps not as 'powerful' as Rogers first suggested. What is much less clear is what exactly happens in these groups, and how this creates these effects. Systematic research on these questions is available but has not yet provided very clear answers.[12]

My own rather limited experience of groups of this type (mainly T Groups) does suggest that they can develop a structure and atmosphere which enables members to experiment and change. For example, in one group I attended over a few days one of the members (I shall call him Tony) stood up in a very determined way in one of the later sessions and said that he would like to say something. Everyone said 'OK', quietly wondering what was so serious that Tony had to make what seemed like a formal speech. Then Tony said 'I'm a diabetic', and sat down hastily. He looked as though he was waiting for us all to hurl abuse at him! Of course, nobody did – we simply asked him why he had felt the need to make that statement. It turned out that, because he had perceived a social stigma in being a diabetic (this was over twenty years ago), he had concealed it from friends and family for nearly twenty years. This was the first collection of people he had felt able to discuss it with since his diagnosis. You could almost feel his relief at being accepted in the group despite this 'revelation' and we then discussed how he could reveal it to his family in the most appropriate way.

This anecdote illustrates that groups can offer the support which enables members to discuss issues and feelings which are very deeply held or possibly painful. And it shows how important is the role of communication in these groups.

What can happen in these groups?

There are a number of processes in these groups which we can relate back to previous chapters:

Stages of development

There is no doubt that these groups tend to follow the developmental trends which were identified by Tuckman.

Developing norms

As suggested above the group can develop norms of trust and 'openness' which can lead to significant self-disclosure.

Feedback

The importance of feedback has already been mentioned with regard to T Groups and this becomes even more critical in groups where more intense group dynamics or interpersonal issues can be revealed.

Confrontation

In everyday life, this term often has a negative connotation implying conflict. The idea in these groups is to make individuals aware of the possibly unrealised implications of their behaviour by 'confronting' them with an interpretation which they can assess and act upon, using the guidelines for good feedback to avoid unnecessary conflict.[13]

What do people get out of them?

Participants certainly report that they have gained in self-awareness, communication skills and group skills and there is external evidence to suggest that these benefits are real. There is also the issue of how these group experiences relate to the participants' everyday lives and what they might mean in a broader social context.[14] What also emerged from the research was that not everyone benefits and this became the focal point of a storm of controversy in the late 1970s which was fuelled by the speculation that these groups were possibly dangerous, especially when they were run by irresponsible trainers.

What do 'trainers' do?

One of the most lengthy reviews of the processes and impact of a whole range of these groups came in 1973 from Lieberman and colleagues.[15] They observed that group leaders would carry out some combination of the following four basic functions:

- emotional stimulation, where the trainer reveals his/her own emotions and stimulates other members to do the same
- caring, where the trainer shows concern and support for group members
- meaning attribution, where the trainer helps members understand the group processes

- executive, where the trainer orders the events and manages the time

Using these functions, they then demonstrated that certain trainers had certain profiles. For example, they distinguished between the 'energiser' who was high on *all* functions and the 'provider' who was moderate on emotional stimulation and executive functions and high on caring and meaning attribution. When they looked at people who felt that they had experienced some psychological harm in the groups they studied, they found that this was associated with energiser group leaders.

Although their general conclusion was that these groups were beneficial, it was this suggestion of possible psychological damage which received the publicity. As a result, this part of their study became the most quoted in the debate which raged over the next few years about the potential advantages and disadvantages of these experiential groups, raising issues such as:

- What were their legitimate goals? How deeply should we reveal our emotions to others within this sort of experience?
- Which techniques were valid? There is no doubt that some of the exercises used by some trainers were very 'powerful' in the emotional reactions they elicited. Did they lead to any valid learning by the group members?
- Should trainers have formal qualifications? Who should be trusted to lead an experiential group? If there is some danger of psychological abuse, would qualified trainers be an adequate safeguard?
- Won't these groups become 'lifestyle' accessories? These groups can (and frequently do) lead to important personal insights. But aren't these insights only really valuable if they are taken over into our daily lives? There were some tales of groups being used by some members as a form of leisure or entertainment, divorced from their everyday experience.
- Weren't these groups 'anti-intellectual'? The emphasis on personal feelings was interpreted as an attack on the validity of intellectual thinking by some observers. There was also a raft of other criticisms which could be interpreted as a 'moral panic' where these groups were accused of being a Communist plot, a threat to democratic values and other exaggerated ills.[16]

What's happening now?

After the explosion of interest in these group experiences in some parts of the USA in the 1960s and 1970s, the optimism associated with them and the associated sub-cultures started to wane. Partly as a result of the association with particular life-styles and values, they never received the systematic research investigation which might have provided more definitive explanations of their impact and effects. But despite this lack of critical attention, it is a mistake to ignore the ideas and techniques which emerged from them for several reasons.

The subculture lives

There is still a lively subculture both in the UK and USA which professes the values of the so-called Human Potential movement and continues to promote the use of various forms of experiential group. The range of groups on offer has become both more varied and more eclectic.

The methods have gone mainstream

In terms of more general influence, the developments of the 1960s and 1970s have had a lasting effect in the sense that methods and techniques which were originally developed under the banner of the experiential movement have now become relatively commonplace in more 'mainstream' training and education.[17]

The growth of self-help

In the last thirty years, there has been an enormous growth in the numbers and membership of self-help groups and organisations with estimates of increasing growth up to around ten million or more individuals in the USA by 1999.[18] Everyone is probably familiar with some of these, such as Alcoholics Anonymous or Gamblers Anonymous, but there is now a self-help or support group to help in most of the misfortunes which can befall us in our everyday routine. To illustrate the range I recently came across a magazine article which surveyed four groups which were started by people involved in the condition they represented, ranging from the UFO Witness Support Group to the Anaphylaxis Campaign.[19] For example, this latter campaign supports parents whose children suffer from allergic reactions to foods which can be fatal. One of the founders lost his daughter, who was allergic to peanuts, when she inadvertently ate a tiny amount of crushed peanut in a lemon meringue pie, collapsed and died due to anaphylactic shock. Within a year, this campaign had 11,000 members and 21 regional groups.

Although there is a tremendous variety of such organisations, they do share many common characteristics. For example, all these groups attempt to provide support and/or bring about personal change in their members. The obvious example of this process is Alcoholics Anonymous who aim to develop their members' acceptance of their problem and then develop a new life-style to cope with it.

Common factors can be identified with other groups which have already surfaced in my discussion of experiential groups:

- importance of group identity
- mutual care and support – 'you are not alone'
- sharing of experience and learning
- common problems or circumstances

There is now a growing research literature on these groups with several promising accounts of how and why they work. For example, Lieberman[20] suggests that four requirements are necessary for positive outcomes:

- group cohesiveness
- saliency
- cognitive restructuring
- diversity of experience

Back to the beginning

In a way, this final example of research brings us back to the beginning of this book where I was arguing that we needed systematic research to help us understand how groups work so that we can use this knowledge to 'make better groups'. This last chapter also demonstrates that small groups can offer an environment in which people can develop new and innovative behaviour.

It also demonstrates that communication plays a crucial role in small group behaviour. A group can become a vehicle for social support and individual development if it develops the appropriate norms and patterns. On the other hand, we have seen the dangers where communication is allowed to develop a dogmatic and authoritarian pattern.

Final thoughts

This book has tried to review the main processes which are important when we try to understand how groups interact and communicate. However, there is still an awful lot left to discover about the workings (or not) of the groups we join in our daily lives. Recently, Michael West complained that:

> there are few clear and authoritative overviews available which describe what is known and what is not known about human behaviour in groups in work settings.[21]

Although I have tried to contribute something of an overview of important things we know and which we can apply, there are still many areas of relatively unexplored territory as the following examples illustrate:

Mysterious meetings

In the early 1970s, Henry Mintzberg undertook probably the most famous study of how managers actually spent their day (as opposed to what theorists said they should be doing).[22] He found that managers spent nearly 70 per cent of their day in scheduled and unscheduled meetings (nearly 60 per cent in scheduled meetings) and this finding has been generally supported in subsequent studies. Despite this enormous investment of time and energy in meetings, a recent review was still able to conclude that they were relatively under-studied – we know relatively little about what really goes on in the different types of meeting.[23] Consult your local library shelves and you will find quite a few books about meetings, but virtually all will be written from a practitioner's point of view based on their own, possibly limited, experience.[24]

Encouraging diversity in groups

If research on minority influence and other factors suggests we should encourage diversity in groups, how do we create such diversity and how much diversity is appropriate? For organisational teams, Brewer has suggested the technique of 'cross-cutting' to separate those attributes related to the task from attributes associated with relationships.[25] To take a simple example, suppose we want a project team with representatives from engineering and personnel. Putting two male engineers together with two female personnel specialists would not work according to Brewer as this composition does *not* cross-cut. However, this technique is so new that we do not know how far it works and how far it can be generalised.[26]

Which variable is the most important?

Of the factors reviewed in this book, which are the *most* important barriers to communication in group problem-solving? According to a group of experienced managers surveyed by Broome and Fulbright, the most important factors were deficiencies in procedures and strategy, cultural diversity leading to bias and prejudice, and poor planning.[27] Is this true of other groups in other contexts, such as students groups? For example, communication barriers have been critical in some student groups I have met, whereas this is down to around eighth position in the managers' priorities. In short, we still do not know enough about different types of everyday groups.

The importance of context

Even where we can apply general principles of group dynamics we must also look out for the different ways that these principles are expressed in different contexts. For example, consider the variety of signs and symbols used by street gangs to reinforce their identity and stake out their territory, ranging from specific slang expressions through elaborate graffiti to often quite subtle nonverbal signals. The casual observer may not recognise the style of lacing or make of tennis shoes or the mode of crossing arms which is a clear 'badge' of membership to the neighbourhood youth. How does this range of 'densely coded and deliberately opaque' communication practices compare with methods used in other groups and communities to deal with similar underlying issues of membership and boundary?[28] Edelman and Frey's very moving account of life in a residential facility for people with AIDS shows how the community has developed a wide range of rather formal practices for integrating new members, including pre-entry visits, a residents' council, weekly house meetings and a buddy system where newcomers are paired with a veteran resident for their first few weeks.[29] The emphasis here is on formal rules and procedures rather than the more implicit and 'coded' communication of gangland. Of course, communication in this community also has many symbolic elements such as the language used to represent death – the word 'death' is hardly ever used and expressions like 'passing on' are preferred. There are also symbolic events such as a balloon ceremony to mark the passing of a resident.

Moving forward

On the basis of this 'great unknown', I shall repeat my advice from Chapter 1 that all the ideas and findings in this book should be treated as hypotheses to apply to the group situations in which you find yourself, in the same way that a scientist will apply a hypothesis to a situation. If it does not seem to work then use some of the other ideas in this book to see if you can explain what is going on.

And do not forget the importance of people's feelings and what might be lurking 'under the surface' of the behaviour in question. One last example from the work of Tom Douglas will illustrate this point. He tells the tale of the young male in a group of patients recently discharged from a psychiatric unit. The young man always treated the situation in a very light-hearted way which earned him relentless abuse and ridicule from the other more serious-minded members of the group. Despite this abuse, he refused either to change his behaviour or stop attending. When he was asked why he persevered despite this torrent of abuse, he revealed the importance of his 2 hours in the group each week where he was the centre of attention. This was much more satisfying than the 'isolation and loneliness he would otherwise experience'.[30]

What Douglas does not explain is why the group did not seek out the reasons for this young man's behaviour and try to help. And this points to the final message of this book. In the previous chapters, I have tried to point out the practical implications of the theory and research findings on the grounds that we can reflect on our group interaction and choose to behave differently if we wish. Perhaps this reflection is the one critical process. Certainly it is the process which forms the conclusion to the most impressive recent overview of workgroup research. This argues that the effectiveness, member well-being, and social processes of a decision-making group will depend upon that group's 'task reflexivity', defined as:

the extent to which group members overtly reflect upon the group's objectives, strategies and processes, and adapt them to current or anticipated endogenous or environmental circumstances.[31]

Of course, the success of this reflection will depend on communication. As they say on many quiz and game shows, the choice is yours.

Notes

1 This quote is from page 5 of an excellent overview of the early development of experiential groups and their impact: Smith, P. B., (ed.) (1980) *Small Groups and Personal Change*. London: Methuen.
2 The process and leadership of small groups in therapeutic contexts is discussed in Posthuma's book, which also provides an interesting discussion of relevant leader skills: Posthuma, B. (1996) *Small Groups in Counselling and Therapy*. 2nd edn. Massachusetts: Allyn and Bacon.
3 For example, see some of the work by Tom Douglas: Douglas, T. (1993) *A Theory of Groupwork*. London: Macmillan.
4 If you want to explore these origins, see: Moreno, J. L. (1970) The Viennese origins of the encounter movement, paving the way for existentialism, group psychotherapy and psychodrama. *Group Psychotherapy*, 22, 7–16.
5 For an early discussion of the therapeutic community notion, see: Jones, M. (1953) *The Therapeutic Community*. New York: Basic Books.
6 One of the best overviews of the early T Groups and the later developments is: Blumberg, A. and Golembiewski, R. T. (1976) *Learning and Change in Groups*. Harmondsworth: Penguin.
7 See Chapter 8 of Aronson's classic text which is now into its 7th edition, and: Aronson, E. (1973) *The Social Animal*. London: Routledge and Kegan Paul.
8 For discussion of this and other issues, see the text by Golembiewski and Blumberg: Golembiewski, R. T. and Blumberg, A. (eds) (1970) *Sensitivity Training and the Laboratory Approach*. Itasca, IL: F. E. Peacock.
9 See Chapter 8 of the book by Peter Smith (note 1).
10 See pages 45ff. of Blumberg and Golembiewski (note 6) for discussion of the variety of encounter groups.
11 The most accessible explanation of Carl Rogers' ideas and methods in this area is: Rogers, C. (1970) *Encounter Groups*. New York: Harper and Row.
12 For an interesting discussion of why these groups became so popular in terms of social trends, see the work of Kurt Back: Back, K. W. (1972) *Beyond Words: The story of sensitivity training and the encounter movement*. New York: Russell Sage Foundation; Back, K. W. (1973) The experiential group and society. *Journal of Applied Behavioural Science*, 9, 7–20; Back, K. W. (ed.) (1978) *In Search of Community: Encounter groups and social change*. Boulder, CO: Westview Press.

13 An interesting discussion of confrontation can be found in Posthuma, pages 122–3. (note 2 above).

14 For example, see the work of Kurt Back (note 12).

15 Be wary of secondhand accounts of this study as they often focus on the 'damages' chapter rather than the balanced overview: Lieberman M. A., Yalom, I. D. and Miles, M. B. (1973) *Encounter Groups: First facts*. New York: Basic Books.

16 See Chapter 8 of Blumberg and Golembiewski (note 6).

17 For example, see the range of publications produced for group facilitators since the 1970s by Pfeiffer & Company, including the Annuals (containing experiential learning activities, questionnaires and inventories, and articles) and the Encyclopaedia of Group Activities, both edited by J. William Pfeiffer.

18 See Chapter 14 of Posthuma (note 2).

19 The article was in the January 1995 issue of Sainsbury's magazine.

20 See in: Lieberman, M. A. (1990) A group therapist perspective on self-help groups. *International Journal of Group Psychotherapy*, 40, 251–78.

21 See page xv of Michael West's important overview: West, M. (ed.) (1996) *Handbook of Work Group Psychology*. Chichester: John Wiley.

22 This text became a managerial 'classic': Mintzberg, H. (1973) *The Nature of Managerial Work*. New York: Harper and Row.

23 This study also established a typology of management meetings: Volkema, R. J. and Niederman, F. (1995) Organizational Meetings. Formats and information requirements. *Small Group Research*, 26, 3–24.

24 One honourable exception is the work by John Tropman, based on the Meeting Masters Research Project, although even here we can question how representative this research has been: Tropman, J. E. (1996) *Making Meetings Work*. Thousand Oaks, CA: Sage.

25 For fuller details of Brewer's technique, see: Brewer, M. B. (1996) Managing diversity: can we reap the benefits without paying the costs? In Jackson, S. E. and Ruderman, M. (eds) *Diversity in Workteams: Paradigms for a changing workplace*. Washington, DC: American Psychological Association.

26 See Chapter 3 by Susan A. Jackson in West (note 21).

27 This survey produced a model with five levels of factors in decreasing order of importance: Broome, B. J. and Fulbright, L. (1995) A multi-stage influence model of barriers to group problem-solving. A participant-generated agenda for small group research. *Small Group Research*, 26, 25–55.

28 Dwight Conquerhood gives a very detailed analysis of gang communication (quote from page 26) in his contribution to Frey's excellent collection of recent studies of natural groups: Conquerhood, D. (1994) Homeboys and Hoods: Gang communication and cultural space. In Frey, L. R. (ed.) *Group Communication in Context*. Hillsdale, NJ: Lawrence Erlbaum Associates.

29 Chapter 1 of Frey's book (note 28) in his work with Mara B. Edelman on the nature of communication in this residential facility – The Pilgrim

must embark: creating and sustaining community in a residential facility for people with AIDS.

30 See page 128 of: Douglas, T. (1995) *Survival in Groups: The basics of group membership*. Buckingham: Open University Press.

31 See the concluding Chapter 22, page 449, by Michael West in his recent handbook (note 21).

INDEX

Action-Centred Leadership 95–6, 102, 193
acts 35–6, 42, 47
actual productivity 137–8
Adair, J. 95–6, 103
adjourning 55, 57
advice 65, 66
agentic state 118
agreement 85
Alcoholics Anonymous 211, 212
analytic group therapy 42–3
Anaphylaxis Campaign 211–12
anchoring 140–1
anonymity 165, 166, 167
anxiety 62
Apollo syndrome 123, 124
Asch, S.E. 73–8
Ashridge Management College 181
assessment 193
Attila the Hun 89
authoritarian leadership 96–7
authoritative mode 41
authority 113, 115–19
autistic hostility 159
autokinetic phenomenon 72–3
autonomy 83

Bales, R.F.: decision-making 61, 63, 67; Interaction Process Analysis 34–5, 36, 39, 95, 97, 121; SYMLOG 37
Bantel, K.A. 177
basic assumption groups 44–5, 62
basic encounter groups 207
Baumrind, D. 117

Bay of Pigs 148–9, 151
behaviour patterns 159–61
behavioural traps 141
behaviours 105–6, 124
Belbin, R.M. 25–6, 120–6, 127
Benne, K.D. 120
Bennis, W.G. 60, 103, 104
biases 139–41, 214
Bion, W.R. 43–5, 46, 62, 63, 203–4
Blackler, F. 182
Blake, R.R. 97, 100–1
blame 5
Blanchard, K.H. 100
blocking 14
Borough, M. 15
boys' clubs 96–7, 106
brainstorming 11–16
brainwashing 167
Bramley, W. 199
Brewer, M.B. 213–14
Bristol 167–8
Broome, B.J. 214
Brown, R. 21
Brown, R.J. 31
Brown, S. 190
BTEC 192
Business Process Re-engineering (BPR) 178
bystander intervention 79–81

Camp David Summit 61
caring function 209
Carr, S. 166–7
Carter, Jimmy 61
case conferences 36–7

categorisation 20–1, 163–4, 168–9
censorship 11–12, 13
Challenger disaster 7–9
chaos 66–7
Charge of the Light Brigade 147
charismatic leadership 94
China 101
Churchill, Winston 89
Cissna, K.N. 62–3, 66
coercive power 113
cognitive restructuring 212
coherent profiles 126
cohesion 54, 150–1, 212
Cold War 147
collectivism 31
commitment 57
common enemy 161
common fate 20
common sense 10–11
communication 6, 39–40;
    intergroup 159, 170–1; and
    leadership 103–4; and problem-
    solving 141–2; and structure
    127–9
communication problems 34
competences 104–5
competition 162
competitive groups 31
compliance 82, 117–18, 166–7
conflict: in group development 54,
    57; intergroup 156, 158–9, 161–
    2, 169; minority influence 84;
    student groups 191, 195–7
conflict breakpoints 67
conformity 6, 71–2, 165;
    autokinetic phenomenon 72–3;
    bystander intervention 79–81;
    factors 81–2; group decision 78–
    9; unanimous majority 73–8
confrontation 209
confused profiles 126
Conquerhood, D. 88–9
consensual validation 81–2
consensus 131–2, 145, 146, 197
consideration 95
consistency 83
context 30–1, 214–15; *see also*
    cultural background
contingency models 99–101

contingency theory 97–9
control 34
convergent thinking 84
conversion theory 83–4
co-operation 30, 31
counterdependency 64, 66
Coverdale Organisation 194
Creative Problem Solving (CPS) 15
creator innovator 127
criticism 205
cross-cutting 213–14
Cuba 148–9
cults 29
cultural background 21–2, 30–1,
    171; leadership 101, 106–7
cultural diversity 214
culture 31, 104
Cunningham, I. 193
Cushman, D.P. 171
Custer, General 147

Danziger, K. 38, 39–40
Darley, J.M. 80–1
decision-making 131–5, 151–2;
    alternatives 143–6; defective 1–7,
    146–51
decision problems 34
deindividuation 118, 165–6, 167,
    168
Delphi 144, 146
democratic leadership 96–7
dependency (basic assumption type)
    44, 45
dependency (stage) 63–4, 65, 66
desirable behaviours 35, 37, 41, 42
destructive behaviours 35, 36, 37,
    41, 42
diagnosis 68
dialectic decision-making 146
dictator decision-making 146
diffused responsibility 166
disasters 1–9, 147
discordant profiles 126
discrimination 157, 162
diversity 212, 213–14
Dixon, N. 147
dominant behaviour 37
double bind dilemmas 107
double minorities 84, 85

Douglas, T. xi, 24, 193, 215
Drew, S. 192–3
Dulewicz, V. 125
dyads 21

Edelman, M.B. 214–15
Education for Capability 192
effectiveness 123–4, 126–7, 131
Egypt 61
emotional attachment 21
emotional stimulation 209
emotions 48
empowerment 183
encounter groups 203, 206–8
energisers 210
Enk, G. 15
Enterprise in Higher Education 192
entrapment 159, 161
episodes 47
equilibrium theory 61–2
Esalen Institute 206
ethics 117, 118
evaluation 21; brainstorming 11,
    14; group socialisation 57
evaluation problems 34
executive function 210
experiential groups *see* groupwork
expert power 113

facilitative mode 41
Falbo, T. 113–14
Falklands war 78
family groups 25
feedback xi, 204, 205, 209
Fiedler, F.E. 97–9, 102
fight/flight 44
Finkelstein, S. 177
flight 64, 66
folly 147
Fonda, H. 134
football 90
forming 54, 56, 205
Foulkes, S.H. 42–3
Fraser, C. 22, 23, 25
free riders 14
Freud, S. 62
Frey, L.R. 214–15
friendly behaviours 35, 37, 41, 42
friendship groups 25

Fulbright, L. 214
functional analysis 39–40
fundraising groups 65
Furnham, A. 13, 125

Gamblers Anonymous 211
gangs 88–9, 214–15
Gardner, H. 103–4
gender 9, 107
Genovese, Kitty 79–80
Ghandi, M. 104
Gibbs, G. 190
goals 55, 60, 142–3, 161, 210
Griffiths, M. 194
group boundaries 22
group cohesion 54, 150–1, 212
group content 24; *see also* tasks
group culture 63
group decisions 78–9
group definition 19–26
group development 53–4; *see also*
    stages
group effectiveness 123–4, 126–7,
    131
group identification 28–9, 81, 162
group identity 212
group innovation 144–5
group interaction 20; categories
    22–4; integrative model 29–31;
    and problem-solving 141–2
group loyalty 31, 78; initiation
    procedures 59; Japan 29, 30
group maintenance 61–2, 100–1,
    120
group members, maturity 100
group mind 168
group norms 20, 23, 71; extremity
    82; groupwork 208; and identity
    168
group performance 135–7, 141–2;
    disastrous 146–51
group polarisation 148
group processes 24, 136; classifying
    24–5; problems 138
group productivity 21–2
group roles 6–7, 23, 104–5, 120–7
group size 21
group socialisation 57–9
group teaching 192–7

groupthink 148–51
groupwork 202–3, 211–12; origins
    203–4; processes 208–9; trainers
    209–10; *see also* encounter
    groups; T Groups
Gudykunst, W.B. 170–1

Hackman, J.R. 179
Hall, J. 132–3
Hardingham, A. 68
Hare, A.P. 61
Hart, S. 15
Heron, J. 39, 40–1
Hersey, P. 100
heuristics 140
hierarchies 185–6
higher education (HE) 189–90
high-performance teams 181
Hinkle, S. 31
Hirokawa, R. 8
histories 47
hitch-hiking 12
Hogg, M.A. 150–1
housewives 78–9
Human Potential movement 211

ice-breakers 16
ideas 11–12, 13
identification 62
identity 168
image 101–2
imbalance 122–3, 124
implementors 107
inclusion 64, 66
independence 75–6
India 106
individual performance 135–6,
    141–2
individualism 31
inequalities 185–6
informational influence 76–7
initiating structure 95
initiation 58–9
innovation 82
innovators 107
intensity 39
interaction *see* group interaction
Interaction Process Analysis (IPA)
    34–6, 121; difficulties and issues

38–9; group development 61–2;
    usage 36–7
intergroups 168–71; conflict
    157–68, 195–6; definition 156–7
interpersonal-group continuum
    27–8, 169, 170
interpersonal underworld 29, 182
Interplace 125
interpretation 42, 48
interventions 68–9; student groups
    197–9; team-building 183–4
investment 83
Israel 61

Jamieson, K.H. 107
Janis, I. 148–51
Japan: friendship formation 171;
    group loyalty 29, 30; leadership
    21–2, 90, 100–1, 106
Jaques, D. 192
Jaques, E. 184–5
John XXIII 104
juries 133–5

Kanter, M.R. 185–6
Katzenbach, J.R. 178, 180–1, 198
Kennedy, John 89
King, D.C. 141
King, Martin Luther 89
King, S.S. 171
Knight, P. 190
knowledge gap 186
Kuhn, M.H. 26

labelling 125–6
laboratory groups 25
laissez-faire leadership 96
Latané, B. 80–1, 146
laterality 113
leaders: advice for 65, 66; changing
    role 60; groupwork 204–5, 209;
    six-category intervention analysis
    40–1
leadership 88–9, 91, 108;
    assumptions 89–91; contingency
    approaches 97–101; cultural
    variations 21–2; folly 147;
    functions 94–6; and image
    101–2; and management 102–3,

184–5; and personality 92–4; and power 114–15; research 103–7; self-directed teams 179; styles 6, 96–7, 196–7; team roles 123
leadership training 101–2
learning grids 194
Least Preferred Co-worker (LPC) scale 97–9
Leavy, B. 91
legitimate power 113
Levine, J.M. 57–9
Lewin, K. 78–9, 96–7, 204
Lieberman, M.A. 209–10, 212
liking 119–20
Lippitt, R. 96–7
Little Big Horn 147
Long, S. 45–6
Lord, R.G. 92, 94

McCann, R. 127
McCarthy, J. 77
McPartland, T.S. 26
maintenance 61–2, 100–1
management 102–3
management teams 120–1
Managerial Grid 97, 100–1, 102
managerial leadership 184–5
managers 213
Mann 92, 94
Marchington, M. 185
Margerison, C. 127
Marshall, P. 193
maturity 100
meaning attribution 209
meetings 213
mental abilities 124
Michaelson, L.K. 141–2
Milgram, S. 115–19, 165, 167
military catastrophes 147, 148–9
Miller, C. xiv
minority influence 82–5
Mintzberg, H. 103, 213
Misumi, J. 100–1, 106–7
monocultural groups 9
moral character 101
Moreland, R.L. 57–9
Moreno, J.L. 119–20, 203
Moscovici, S. 82–5, 148
Mouton, J.S. 97, 100–1

multicultural groups 9
My Lai massacre 118–19

Nanus, B. 104
Napoleon 89
NASA 7, 8
National Training Laboratories (NTL) 205–6
negative behaviours 35, 36, 37, 41, 42
negative roles 122
negative stereotyping 169
negotiation 27–8, 169, 170
Nelson, H. 103
Nemeth, C.J. 84
Nemiroff, P.M. 141
network experiments 127–8
networking 103–4
nominal group technique (NGT) 144
nonverbal communication 206; observation 35–6, 38, 42, 47
normative influence 76–7
norming 54, 56
norms see group norms
Nottingham Trent University 194

observation systems 47, 55, 65
Ohio State leadership studies 95, 97
open-mindedness 83
Organisation Development (OD) 206
organisational design 182–3
organisations 177–8, 184–7; culture 8; effective teams 179–82; T Groups 206; team-building 182–4; team structures 178–9
Osborn, A.F. 11, 13
outdoor activities 184, 194

pacifiers 107
pairing 44
Parsons, D.E. 192–3
Parsons, T. 60–1
Pavitt, C. 146
perceptions 126, 204
PERFORM 68
performance 100–1
performance ethic 181, 198

Performance-Maintenance
    leadership theory 100–1
performing 55, 56
Perrin, S. 77–8
personal identity 26–7
personal learning 206
personality 6–7, 92–4, 104–5, 147
Peters, T.J. 104
Peterson, M.F. 21–2, 91, 101, 105
planned team development 67–9
Plymouth Business School 193–4
PM leadership theory 100–1
Poole, M.S. 67
position power 98
positive behaviours 35, 37, 41, 42
Posthuma, B. 203
potential productivity 137–8
potential teams 180
power 114–15, 169
power relationships 164
power structures 113–14
prejudice 157, 214
pride 30
Principle of Minimal Sufficiency
    166–7
prisons 164–7
problem-solving 11, 138–43,
    151–2; alternative 143–6; and
    communication 141–2;
    communication barriers 214;
    group goals 142–3
problem-solving groups 55, 61–2
procedures 6, 30, 214
processes see group processes
production blocking 14
productivity see group performance
project groups 192
providers 210
pseudo-teams 180
psychoanalysis 42–6, 203–4
psychodrama 203
psychological closeness 63
psychological distinctiveness 163
psychological safety 145

Quinn, R.E. 104–5

rationality 113
real teams 181

recycling 67
referent power 81, 113
Reicher, S. 167–8
reintegration 34
resource problems 138
resources 136, 137, 186
reward power 113
Ringelmann effect 135
riots 167–8
risky shifts 147–8
rituals 58–9
Robber's Cave Experiment 158–9
Roberts, A. 193
Robinson, M. 46
Rodrigues, C.A. 107
Rogers, C. 206–8
role demands 6–7, 166, 190
role-playing 203
role transition 58
roles 104–5, 120–7
Roth, R. A. 67
Rowland, D. 194
Royal, J. 68
rules 11–12

Saavedra, R. 84–5
saliency 212
scapegoating 45–6
scholarship of teaching 190
schoolchildren 29, 194
Schutz, W. 206
science 82
Sedwick, J. 147
selective perception 139
self-categorisation 20–1, 163–4,
    168–9
self-concept 26–7, 168
self-destruction 28–9
self-development groups 29, 40–1;
    see also T-groups
self-directed teams (SDTs) 178–9,
    198–9
self-esteem 163
self-help groups 211–12
self-study groups 26, 203–4
seminar groups 190–1
seniority gap 186
sensitivity training 203, 204–6
Shackleton, V. 107

Shambaugh, P.W. 63
Shea, M. 90–1, 93, 96, 114–15
Sheats, P. 120
Sheffield Hallam University 192
Shepard, H.A. 60
Sherif, C.W. 157–9, 161–2
Sherif, M. 156–7; autokinetic
    phenomenon 72–3; summer
    camps 157–9, 161–2, 164, 169
Shimmin, S. 182
Silverlock, M. 189
Silverlock, T. 189
situational control 98
situational leadership 100
six-category intervention analysis
    40–1
Skillpacks 192
skills 105–6, 127
Smith, D.K. 178, 180–1, 198
Smith, P.B. 21–2, 26, 91, 105, 202
Sniezek, J.A. 146
social background 30–1
social categorisation 163
social comparison 80, 81, 163
social conformity see conformity
social contact 161
social control 169
social definition 81
social emotional area 34, 35
social identity 26, 163, 168–9
social identity theory 169, 171
social influence 71–2
social process interventions 184,
    198
social situation 166
social structure 20
social support 81–2
social systems 34
social work groups 203
socio-emotional behaviours 34–5,
    95–6, 97–8
sociometry 119–20
Spencer, C. 77–8
staff 190, 191, 198–9
stages 11–12, 65, 66, 208; criteria
    64–5; diagnosis 68; problem-
    solving 143; sequences 54–62;
    team development 181–2
Stanford Prison Simulation 164–7

status 6, 114–15
Steiner, I.D. 138–9, 141
Stephenson, G. 169, 170, 171
stereotyping 168–9
stimulus ambiguity 82
Stogdill, R.M. 92
Stoner, J.A.F. 147–8
storming 54, 56
street gangs 88–9, 214–15
strength 113
stress 150–1
Strodtbeck, F.L. 61, 67
structure (of group) 127–9
structure (stage) 64, 66
structured problem-solving 143
stuckness 64
student groups 189, 190–2; group
    teaching 192–5; interventions
    195–9
subjective uncertainty 82
submissive behaviour 37
substance 93
suicide 29
summer camps 157–9, 161–2, 164,
    169
superordinate goals 161
surveillance 82
Svetlik, I. 176–7, 178, 179
Swift, K. xiv
SYMLOG (System for the Multiple
    Level Observation of Groups)
    37–8

T Groups 60, 182, 204–6, 208
Tajfel, H.: group definition 21, 22,
    23, 25, 169; minimal groups
    162–4
task demands 136, 137–8
task groups 60–1
task problems 34, 35, 138, 184
task reflexivity 215–16
tasks 30; classification 136–7;
    flipping 61–2; and leadership
    95–6, 97–8
Tavistock Institute 44, 203–4
Taylor, D.S. 105–6
teachers 190, 191, 198–9
team-building 182–4, 198
Team Climate Inventory 145

team innovation 144–5
Team Management System (TMS) 127
teams 67, 177–8, 186–7; effective 179–82; inequalities 185–6; roles 120–7; structures 178–9; *see also* planned team development
tension 156, 169, 195–7
tension reduction 34
termination (stage) 64
Tetlock, P.E. 150
Thatcher, M. 101, 103, 104
therapeutic groups 43–5, 206–7
therapists 206
therapy groups 55, 61, 63, 202–3
think-tank groups 123, 124
thinking styles 84
Three Mile Island 139
thruster organiser 127
Tjosvold, D. 182–3
Townsend, R. 103, 104
trainers 205, 209–10
training: Creative Problem Solving 15; leaders 101–2
training groups *see* T groups
traps 141
Trekkies 27
trust (stage) 64, 66
Tuckman, B.W.; stages 54–7, 61, 68, 205, 208
tug-of-war teams 135, 137
Turner, J.C. 21
Twelve Angry Men 134

UFO Witness Support Group 211
unanimous majority 73–8, 81–2
uncertainty 54, 55, 57, 82
uncompetitive groups 31
UNESCO 190
unfriendly behaviours 35, 36, 37, 41, 42

United Kingdom 192; conformity 78; groupwork 211; higher education 189–90; leadership 21–2, 90, 95
United States 30, 78–9; conformity 77–8; friendship formation 171; groupwork 211; leadership 21–2, 90, 96

valuable roles 122
values 104
Van Dynne, L. 84–5
Vaughan, D. 8
verbal transcripts 35–6, 38, 47
vision 102, 103–4, 180, 182–3

Waterman, R.H. 104
Watson 132
Wellings, R.S. 178–9
West, M. 213, 215–16; effective teams 179–80; team-building 183–4; team innovation 144–5
Wheelan, S. 63–5, 66
White, R.K. 96–7
Whyte, W.F. 114
Williams, S. 107
Wilson, D. 91
women 107
Woodcock, M. 181–2
Worchel, S. 65, 66
work groups 25, 29, 44–5, 62
work (stage) 64, 66
working groups 180
worthwhile behaviours 35, 37, 41, 42
Wright, P.L. 105–6

Zander, A. 30
Zimbardo, P.G. 164–7, 169